THE CHINESE WALL

PLAYS BY MAX FRISCH
(Published by Hill and Wang)

The Chinese Wall
The Firebugs
Andorra
Biography: A Game
Max Frisch: Three Plays
Don Juan, or The Love of Geometry
The Great Rage of Philip Hotz
When the War Was Over

THE CHINESE WALL

(*Die Chinesische Mauer*)

A Farce by **MAX FRISCH**

Translated by
JAMES L. ROSENBERG
Introduction by
HAROLD CLURMAN

A *Spotlight Dramabook*
HILL AND WANG — NEW YORK

Standard Book Number (clothbound edition): 8090-3430-1
Standard Book Number (paperback edition): 8090-1203-0

Library of Congress catalog card number 61-16870

FIRST DRAMABOOK EDITION SEPTEMBER 1961
SECOND PRINTING SEPTEMBER 1965
THIRD PRINTING AUGUST 1967
FOURTH PRINTING FEBRUARY 1969

Manufactured in the United States of America by the
Colonial Press, Clinton, Mass.

MAX FRISCH

Born in 1911 in Zurich (and thus old enough to have lived through two world wars), Max Frisch has been for some fifteen years one of the outstanding literary figures in Europe. That he has remained up until this time almost totally unknown in America is partly a result of his own lack of interest in a world-wide reputation, but is probably more particularly a commentary on the present state of the theatre in America. Even Frisch's equally distinguished fellow-countryman, Friedrich Duerrenmatt, has at least enjoyed a sort of *succés de scandale* on Broadway with his *The Visit*, but *The Chinese Wall*—written in 1946 and revised in 1955—is the first Frisch play to be translated and published in America.

Frisch is—and has been throughout his adult life—an architect by profession, a writer by avocation, which may account for his persistent experimentalism and his indifference to commercial considerations. His style, as exemplified in *The Chinese Wall*, is obviously indebted to Brecht, but even more to Thornton Wilder, whose *The Skin of Our Teeth* may be seen as the optimistic other side of the coin to Frisch's deeply pessimistic "world theatre" in *The Chinese Wall.*

Although Frisch had written several plays, novels, and stories before he wrote *The Chinese Wall*, it was this play that first brought him fame beyond the borders of Switzerland. Its impact on a world which was still listening to the echoes of Hiroshima and Nagasaki is not hard to imagine. It was followed by several other works exhibiting that peculiar bitter-sweet blend of ironic wit and profound despair that is the trademark of Frisch as a writer—*Graf Oederland* (1951), *Don Juan, oder Die Liebe zur Geometrie* (1953), and *Biedermann und die Brandstifter* (1959).

The latter is a good example of Frisch's indefatigable passion for revision (a passion he shares with Duerrenmatt). Originally written in 1953 as a radio play, it was reworked in 1959 into a stage play, and then in 1960 was re-revised and produced as *Biedermann und Die Hölle*. The "Don Juan" of the play bearing his name originally appeared as a minor character in *The Chinese Wall*. *Graf Oederland* was originally an extended prose sketch in one of Frisch's published diaries.

In addition to his plays, Frisch has published several novels (two of which, *Stiller* and *Homo Faber*, have been translated into English), diaries, and various literary and political essays. He has in recent years received a number of literary prizes. He travels frequently; shortly after World War II, he spent a year in America on a Rockefeller grant.

He is at present living near Zurich and continuing his twin careers of architecture and literature.

—J.R.

JAMES L. ROSENBERG is Professor of Dramatic Literature at the Carnegie Institute of Technology. He has published a volume of poetry, a verse translation of *Sir Gawain and the Green Knight,* translations of plays by Molière, Günter Grass, and Tankred Dorst, and various critical essays. He has also edited, with Robert Corrigan, *The Art of the Theatre* and *The Context and Craft of Drama.*

INTRODUCTION

When I was in Germany in 1958 I was told by a lady busy with the translation, distribution, and production of American plays in various cities there that though the theatre in that country was most active very few new German plays of distinction were being written. The exceptions were the plays of two Swiss writers, Friedrich Duerrenmatt and Max Frisch. We know Duerrenmatt as a dramatist through *The Visit* in which Alfred Lunt and Lynn Fontanne starred. Max Frisch, who was born in 1911, makes his English-language bow here as a playwright with *The Chinese Wall,* which he wrote in 1946 and revised in 1955.

I know of no play which is more universally contemporary than *The Chinese Wall.* And it may be significant that such a play comes from a traditionally noncombatant country surrounded on all sides by nations whose histories may be read as a long series of wars with their aftermaths and the continued anticipation or fear of further wars.

The reason for this anomaly may be that *neutrality* no longer has the sound of safety which characterized the term up to 1945. And the reason I refer to the play's contemporaneity before anything else which distinguishes it is that the central question of our time is not the struggle between East and West or between two ideologies but rather the survival of man. "Europe" says one of the characters in the play "is death," but he is a character out of the past. The "eternal" lovers of history (hence contemporary) realize that "The world's become a single grave."

The subject of the play then is this all-embracing preoccupation of our day, the problem transcending all parties or national issues. Yet the author calls his play—and this too is utterly characteristic—a "farce." It is a farce because of its theatrical form—a morality play in terms of a masquerade, almost a spoof. No realistic illusion is sought: "the stage remains a stage" as the author notes for the director's benefit. Thus it is possible for Hitler to appear as a guest at the inauguration ball of the Chinese Wall (221 B.C.), for a contemporary to converse with Napoleon, Brutus, Don Juan, Columbus—and Cleopatra to sit on a Chinese Emperor's knee. Yet all through this toying with time and history one senses the author's agony over our present dilemma.

Another farcical aspect of the situation is that its horror, which has been so often described (and photographed), still makes relatively little impression. "The end of history" in this country at least still strikes many as so much science fiction, a theme for sensational film exploitation. Many of our "serious" discussions are in fact frivolous, for while they may lead our minds to a view of total extinction no one will actually take its possibility seriously. Our air-raid exercises are more propaganda than precaution.

"We are face to face with the choice: will there be a human race or not? The end of the world can be manufactured. The more we become able to do (thanks to technology) the more nakedly we stand like Adam and Eve before the primal question 'What do we want.' " Thus speaks the Contemporary, the central figure in *The Chinese Wall,* who stands in the midst of the frolic of his arguments, images, quips, stage tricks and diversions somewhat in the manner that we, readers and spectators, occupy our time in diverse entertainments while we rarely turn to the real issue.

During the Thirties most of the ironies of *The Chinese Wall* might have been dubbed "left-wing" stuff. For example, the Chinese Emperor says "We are going to build a wall" and the Contemporary answers "Against the barbarian I know. For the barbarians are always the others . . . and culture, that's always us. And therefore we must liberate other people, for we (and not the others) are the Free World." The Emperor constantly reiterates that he works for Peace—which he defines as "The Great Order [his own regime], the True Order, the Only Order, the Final Order." But in the context of the play these jokes lose all their "radical" color, for the very notion of radicalism or revolution (as the words are ordinarily understood) become absurd: so many delusions which lead to the futile repetition of old follies. We have come to a point of time when a wholly new sort of thinking has become imperative and distinction between right and left are fast becoming almost as obsolete as the chop logic of high-school debating societies.

The author makes merry and even kids his own method (borrowed in part from Brecht, to whom in the course of the play he makes jocular reference), but the play cannot be set down as "hopeful"—for hope in the sense of an abiding optimism would in this connection be tantamount to obscenity. "You have said what you had to say," the Chinese Princess says reassuringly. The Contemporary replies "And achieved nothing." "And still," replies Her Grace, "and still you had to say it."

So *The Chinese Wall*, which is both intelligent and naif, as smiling as a parade and as earnest as a Jeremiad, gentle and mordant, does not conclude with an "answer" or a "solution." It simply bids us attend. As lament or as farce it calls us to *the order of the day*. In this regard, it is less and more than a "play."

HAROLD CLURMAN

The purpose of Spotlight Dramabooks is to introduce single plays by distinguished contemporary authors. For a complete list of these and other Dramabooks (collections of plays and drama criticism), please turn to page 125.

THE CHINESE WALL

CHARACTERS

THE CONTEMPORARY
HWANG TI, *Emperor of China*
MEE LAN, *his daughter*
WU TSIANG, *a Chinese prince*
OLAN, *a Chinese mother*
THE MUTE, *her son*
SIU, *a servant*
DA HING YEN I, II, III, *Masters of the Revels*
FU CHU, *a Chinese executioner*
A HERALD, SOLDIERS, MANDARINS, WAITERS, EUNUCHS, JOURNALISTS
THE MASKERS
- ROMEO and JULIET
- NAPOLEON BONAPARTE
- COLUMBUS
- L'INCONNUE DE LA SEINE
- PONTIUS PILATE
- DON JUAN
- BRUTUS
- PHILIP OF SPAIN
- CLEOPATRA
- MARY STUART
- A GENTLEMAN IN A TAIL COAT
- A GENTLEMAN IN A CUTAWAY

PROLOGUE

The CONTEMPORARY *steps forward in front of a drop curtain on which is painted in realistic style the Chinese Wall.*

THE CONTEMPORARY. Ladies and gentlemen. You are looking at the Chinese Wall, the greatest edifice in the history of mankind. It measures (according to the encyclopedia) over ten thousand li, or—to express it more concretely—the distance between Berlin and New York. According to newspaper reports, the structure is in poor condition; recently, indeed, there has been talk of the government's tearing it down, on the ground that here, as it stands, it no longer serves any real purpose. The Chinese Wall (or, as the Chinese say, the Great Wall), planned as a defensive rampart against the barbaric peoples from the steppes of Central Asia, is another one of these constantly repeated attempts to hold back time, to dam up history, and, as we know today, it has not succeeded. Time will not be held back. This great work was completed under the reign of the glorious Emperor Tsin She Hwang Ti, who tonight will personally appear on our stage. As for the remainder of that with which this evening's action is concerned, and so that no false expectations may be aroused, let me read to you the additional characters in our play [*He reads from a list*]: Romeo and Juliet; Philip of Spain; Mee Lan, a Chinese princess; Pontius Pilate; L'Inconnue de la Seine; Alexander the Great—oh, yes, after a consultation with the author, we have changed that: we will present Napoleon instead (in this play, it really makes no difference, and we've got to remember our wardrobe)—so, Napoleon Bonaparte; Brutus; Don Juan Tenorio; Cleopatra; Christopher Columbus.

Two Chinese figures, OLAN *and* WANG, *mother and son, appear.*

In addition, you will see: Miscellaneous People, Courtiers,

Mandarins and Boards of Directors, A Waiter, An Executioner, Eunuchs, Newspaper Reporters——[*The two Chinese bow to him.*]
Yes—what is it?

Olan. I am a Chinese farmer's wife. My name is Olan. I am the eternal mother who plays no part in the great history of the world.

The Contemporary [*Aside*]. Naturally, she says that now, because later, as we shall see, she will play a most decisive role.

Olan. We live in the time of the Great Exalted Emperor, Tsin She Hwang Ti, called the Son of Heaven, he who is always in the right. We come from the land of Chau. We have been on this pilgrimage for a year now. Seven times we came through floods, thirty times we were seized by soldiers, ninety times we lost our way—because there *was* no way. Just look at my poor feet! However, you are an honest man, sir, we can see that, and if you tell us that we are in Nanking——

The Contemporary. We are in Nanking.

Olan. Wang! You hear? [WANG *nods.*] Wang! We're in Nanking! Wang! [OLAN *embraces her son.*]

The Contemporary. Why are you crying?

Olan. A whole year, sir, a long year——

The Contemporary. —you have been on this pilgrimage; I understand.

Olan. Do you know the Yangtse-Kiang?

The Contemporary. In my atlas, yes.

Olan. A whole year's walking straight ahead, then a sharp left; and there you are—our land: a lovely place, sir, a fruitful place, you can believe me, plenty of work for us, plenty of crops for the Emperor. Oats and millet, rice and tobacco, bamboo, cotton, poppies, oh, and we have typhoons there, too, and apes and pheasants——

The Contemporary. I understand. And you've just come here from there?

Olan. We have come here from there.

The Contemporary. What do you want in Nanking?

Olan. Wang! You hear? He asks what we want in Nanking. Wang! He asks that. You hear? [WANG *laughs silently.*] We want to see our Emperor!

The Contemporary. Ah.

Olan. Tsin She Hwang Ti, called the Son of Heaven, he who is always in the right. They say it isn't true.

The Contemporary. What isn't true?

Olan. They say it through the whole land.

The Contemporary. What?

Olan. They say he is no Son of Heaven.

The Contemporary. But rather—?

Olan. A blood-sucking leech.

The Contemporary. Hm.

Olan. A hangman, a murderer.

The Contemporary. Hm.

Olan. "What do we count on the day of victory,
We, the farmers and folk in the land?
We count our dead, we count our dead,
While you jingle your gold in your hand."

The Contemporary. Hm. Hm.

Olan. They go around singing it, you know.

The Contemporary. Who does?

Olan. Whoever has a voice. That is my son over there. My son is mute. He doesn't get it from me.

The Contemporary. Mute?

Olan. Perhaps it's just as well that he is mute. Really, my son, really! There's enough stupid talk in this world simply because people know how to talk. And what's the result? For forty years people have been saying things have got to change. They've got to get better. Justice will come. Peace will come. Have you heard the latest, sir?

The Contemporary. I haven't yet spoken to anyone here in Nanking. [OLAN *whispers in his ear.*] Min Ko?

Olan. That's what they call him. The Voice of the People! But no one has ever seen him. Only his sayings are known. Now the Emperor wants to have him killed. Does that mean that men have been singing the truth for forty years? [*Drum rolls are heard.*] Here they come!

A *Chinese* HERALD *enters, along with a* SOLDIER *with a drum, a* SOLDIER *with a lance, a* SOLDIER *with a footstool for the* HERALD.

Herald. "We, Tsin She Hwang Ti, called the Great Exalted Emperor, the Son of Heaven, he who is always in the right, announce to the dutiful people of our realm the following proclamation: [*Roll of drums.*] Victory is ours. The barbarian hounds of the steppes, our last enemies, have been smashed! The barbarian hounds of the steppes lie, as promised, in the lake of their own blood. The world is ours." [*Drum roll.*]

Olan. Heil. Heil. Heil.

The HERALD *looks at* THE CONTEMPORARY *and waits.*

The Contemporary. Heil. [*Drum roll.*]

Herald. "People of our realm! There remains one last adversary today in our land, a single man, who calls himself the Voice of the People: Min Ko. We will seek him out and find him, even to the remotest corner of our land. His head on the block! And to anyone who is caught repeating his sayings, the same thing will happen: *His* head on the block!" [*Drum roll.*] Long live our Great Exalted Emperor, Tsin She Hwang

Ti, called the Son of Heaven, he who is always in the right.

Olan. Heil. Heil. Heil.

The HERALD *looks at* THE CONTEMPORARY *and waits.*

The Contemporary. Heil.

[*The* HERALD *and the three* SOLDIERS *withdraw as they came, perfectly in step, like mechanical figures.*

Olan. You hear, sir?

The Contemporary. Min Ko, the Voice of the People—his head on the block—. It sounds like a crisis for that party in power, which has conquered everything—except the truth. I understand.

Olan. Come, my son, come!

The Contemporary. One more question——

Olan. I don't know anything, sir, I don't know anything! Come, my son. And thank God you are mute!

[OLAN *and* WANG *exit.*

The Contemporary. So much for the situation in Nanking. You are going to ask, ladies and gentlemen, what is meant by all this? Where is this Nanking today? And who, today, is Hwang Ti, the Son of Heaven, he who is always in the right? And this poor mute boy who can't even say a single "Heil" and Wu Tsiang, the general with the bloody boots, and all the rest —what do they all mean? Who are they? I hope you won't be too upset, ladies and gentlemen, if you don't find any ready answer to this. All that is meant (word of honor!) is the truth, but, once you embrace it, you find it two-edged. [*The first gong.*] On with the play! Place of the action: this stage. Or one might also say: our consciousness. Hence, for example, Shakespeare's characters, who exist only in our consciousness; and Biblical quotations, and so forth. Time of the action: this evening. And thus in an era when the building of Chinese Walls has become, you understand, a farce. [*Second gong.*] Tonight, I play the role of an intellectual. [*Third gong.*]

THE PLAY

SCENE 1

The stage remains a stage: right, an outside staircase in the Chinese manner; left, in the foreground, a group of modern armchairs. Ceremonial music is heard and the voices of an unseen company. After a while (when the spectators have had a chance to get used to the stage) there appears a youthful pair in costumes which every theatergoer would recognize.

SHE. Wilt thou be gone? it is not yet near day.
It was the nightingale and not the lark,
That pierced the fearful hollow of thine ear;
Nightly she sings on yond pomegranate tree.
Believe me, love, it was the nightingale.

He. It was the lark, the herald of the morn—
I must be gone and live, or stay and die.

She. Yond light is not day-light, I know it, I;
Therefore stay yet; thou needst not to be gone.

He. Let me be ta'en, let me be put to death;
I am content, so thou wilt have it so.

She. They come! I hear a sound! Farewell!

He. Farewell!

She. O, thinkst thou we shall ever meet again?

A WAITER *in tails appears, right.*

Waiter. Ladies and gentlemen: the Polonaise is beginning on the terrace. The company awaits your pleasure.

[*He disappears.*

He. If I but knew, dear, where we are—and when!
I shudder at these people here. It seems,
They've all ransacked their closets. Their costumes
Smell of mothballs, and in truth it is
As though they all were dead, and yet they talk
And dance about in circles endlessly
Like tiny figures on a musical clock.

She. What has happened?

He. Time—Time is standing still.

She. Away, my love, away! and let us flee!

A WAITER *in tails appears, left.*

Waiter. Ladies and gentlemen: the Polonaise is beginning the terrace. The company awaits your pleasure.

[*The* WAITER *disappears.*

She. O God, I have an ill-divining soul!

He. I know not what, but something strange has happened.
"Entropy" and "atom": what are these?
Somebody speaks, but no one understands.
"Death by radiation"—what is this?
The Time, my love, the Time is standing still.

She. Send news, my love, each hour, every day!
Too many seconds does the year contain;
Counting them all, I will grow old and die
Before we meet again, love, lip to lip.

He. O Juliet! This night I'll lie with thee.

She. O Romeo! beloved Romeo!

He. How oft when men are at the point of death
Have they been merry! O my love! My wife!
The world's become a single grave. O eyes,
Look, look your last! Arms, take your last
Embrace—thus, with a kiss, I die!

The members of the Polonaise enter, in costumes of every

type: NAPOLEON, CLEOPATRA, DON JUAN, THE MAID OF ORLEANS, FREDERICK THE GREAT, HELEN OF TROY, WALLENSTEIN, MARY STUART, LOHENGRIN, *etc.*

Someone. Here they are: Romeo and Juliet, the classic pair!

ROMEO *and* JULIET *are swept up and carried away by the merry-makers.* NAPOLEON BONAPARTE *remains behind, in half profile, his hand in his white vest.* THE CONTEMPORARY, *also left behind, approaches him respectfully.*

The Contemporary. Excellency! Could I speak to you for a moment?

Napoleon. We are not acquainted with thee, Monsieur.

The Contemporary. That's not surprising, Excellency. We live in different Times. Perhaps it would please you to hear, Excellency, that your fame—and I do not wish to startle you in any way—has survived its first century.

Napoleon. What dost thou say?

The Contemporary. That which concerns my insignificance, Excellency, since I belong to the people who are living on the earth today and who would like to live.

Napoleon. A century? sayst thou. And what—inform me!—has happened since then?

The Contemporary. I *will* inform you, Excellency; that's why I have come. You died, if I mistake not, in the spring of 1821. Yet even today you remain a sort of symbol. Your personality, your profile (the inner and the outer man), your glorious campaigns, and your hand's predilection for concealing itself in your vest, these are known to every educated person—indeed, to every half-educated person, and nowadays that's most of mankind. You are admired, Excellency, and not only in France. Your letters may be read in every library—even the most intimate ones (in facsimile, of course). If I may be explicit, Excellency; we are very well acquainted with you. You belong to those figures who people our brains, and to that degree, as a figure in our thoughts, you are still living—otherwise how could I be speaking to you, Emperor of France?—living and dangerous!

Napoleon. I ask, what is happening? What are the French doing? And the British and the Russians? Tell me that they are at last defeated!

The Contemporary. Excellency——

Napoleon. Russia can be defeated; it was an unusually hard winter when we marched against Russia.

The Contemporary. We all know that very well.

Napoleon. Russia *must* be defeated!

The Contemporary. Excellency——

Napoleon. Europe is the world—!

The Contemporary. No more, Excellency, no more——

Napoleon. Who is the Master of Europe?

The Contemporary. Excellency!

Napoleon. Why dost thou not speak, citizen?

The Contemporary. Excellency—the atom is fissionable!

Napoleon. What does that mean?

The Contemporary. That means—with the troops ready, Excellency, and the generals ready: the next war, which we believe to be inevitable, will be the last.

Napoleon. And who will win it?

The Contemporary. No one. You can't grasp that, Excellency, I know. But it is so: the deluge can now be re-enacted. It remains only for the order to be given, Excellency, which means we are faced with the simple choice, will there be a mankind or not? But who, Excellency, should make this choice: humanity itself—or you?

Napoleon. Thou art a democrat?

The Contemporary. I am worried, yes. We can no longer stand the adventure of absolute monarchy, Excellency, nowhere ever again on this earth; the risk is too great. Whoever sits on a throne today holds the human race in his hand, their whole history, starting with Moses or Buddha, including the Acropolis, the Temple of Maia, Gothic cathedrals, including all of Western philosophy, Spanish and French painting, German music, Shakespeare and this youthful pair: Romeo and Juliet. And included in it all, our children and our children's children. A slight whim on the part of the man on the throne, a nervous breakdown, a touch of neurosis, a flame struck by his madness, a moment of impatience on account of indigestion—and the jig is up! Everything! A cloud of yellow or brown ashes boiling up toward the heavens in the shape of a mushroom, a dirty cauliflower—and the rest is silence—radioactive silence.

Napoleon. Why tellst thou this to us, Napoleon Bonaparte, banished to Saint Helena?

The Contemporary. I don't know, Excellency, if you can grasp what a contemporary has to say to you?

Napoleon. Answer me!

The Contemporary. Why do I come and report to you in your banishment? Quite frankly: You must not return, Excellency, not for a hundred days or even a hundred seconds. The era of great generals (even of a great one like yourself) is past.

Napoleon. And if the people call me?

The Contemporary. They won't. The people want to live.

Napoleon. And what if I tell thee, Monsieur, that thou art wrong? I hear the call of the people day after day.

Laughter in the background. THE CONTEMPORARY *turns to the audience.*

The Contemporary. You see, ladies and gentlemen, how ticklish it is speaking with these great personages who people our brains, these evil spirits out of the bad dream of a history which must not be repeated, and who cannot grasp that which a contemporary has to tell them. However, I will not give up. . . .

A new pair of maskers now enters, an elderly man, seemingly a Spanish seafarer, and a young girl, who, barefooted and in laughing rapture, is dancing along before him.

L'Inconnue. Entrez dans la danse,
Voyez comme on danse,
Sautez, dansez,
Embrassez cell'que vous voudrez!

Columbus. I don't understand it. . . .

L'Inconnue. Entrez dans la danse,
Voyez comme on danse. . . .

COLUMBUS *shakes his head.*

L'Inconnue. It's a party, my friend, a great ball, such as I have envisioned a thousand times behind my closed lids when I couldn't sleep beneath the bridges of the Seine.

Columbus. I don't understand it. . . .

L'Inconnue. I love exciting parties, my friend—the formal gardens, which I have never entered; I love the silk, the music which seems to make all things possible. I love the lives of fine people. All this, you understand, I know only from reading the newspapers.

Columbus. America, they call it. . . .

L'Inconnue. We must hurry, my friend, or we'll miss out on the Polonaise. Give me your arm!

Columbus. America, they call it. America! And so it's not India that I've discovered? Do you understand that? Not India, not the truth! [*The two maskers disappear.*

Napoleon. Who was that?

The Contemporary. Columbus, I think, the old Columbus.

Napoleon. I mean the girl.

The Contemporary. She has no name.

Napoleon. She mentioned the Seine.

The Contemporary. Her life was unknown, Excellency, no one inquired into it. We know only her death mask; it hangs in the shop windows and can be bought at any second-hand store. We call her "L'Inconnue de la Seine."

Napoleon. Does that mean that even this barefooted waif is on the guest list?

The Contemporary. So it seems.

Napoleon. And why haven't we been informed whose guests we are?

The Contemporary. I have already told you, Excellency. Nowadays whoever sits on a throne holds humanity in his hand, the whole kaleidoscopic history of deeds and dreams, Romeo and Juliet, Napoleon Bonaparte, Christopher Columbus, and the rest—and even those who are nameless: "L'Inconnue de la Seine"!

The crack of a whip is heard. A Chinese master-of-ceremonies appears, with a pack of coolies who drag in the throne and place it on the stage. All this is carried out like a swift and flawless military drill—left, right, left, right—while periodically the sharp crack of an invisible whip is heard. Then they all disappear.

Napoleon. What is the meaning of all this chinoiserie?

The Contemporary. That's the throne.

Napoleon. And who are these here . . . ?

From the opposite side there appear two new maskers, who promenade back and forth like men awaiting a ceremonious occasion—at which they are expected; back and forth in casual companionship. They are a Roman and a young Spaniard who impatiently, while he listens, toys with a glove and peers mysteriously about.

Pilate. What is truth? Now in that time it happened that I was the governor of a province which was called in Hebrew Eriz Jisrael——

Don Juan. I know, I know——

Pilate. One fine morning (it was the eve of Passover) they brought him to the place of judgment and I said to them: What kind of complaint bringest thou against this man? The Jews, however, answered and said so on and so forth. Then I went back to him and said to him: Art thou King of the Jews? But he replied: My kingdom is not of this world——

Don Juan. I know!

Pilate. After this, when he had thus spoken, I went to the high priests and said: I find no fault in him. Then they cried and said: He has claimed to be the Son of God! Then, as I heard these words, I was greatly afraid and returned and spoke to him, saying: Whither comest thou? He, however, made no answer. I sat then, in the seat of judgment (that which in Hebrew is called Gabbatha) and waited his answer, but in vain. Everyone that is of the truth heareth my voice, he said; then I said: What is truth?

Don Juan. I know, we all know.

Pilate. However, I am not fond of decisions. How can I decide what is the truth? There was an uproar, though, and before the place of judgment they cried: Crucify him! Crucify him! And I spoke and said: I have a custom of releasing one at Passover. Which do you want me to release? Then they all cried together and said: Not this one, but Barabbas!

Don Juan. I know—I know.

Pilate. Yet, Barabbas was a robber.

Don Juan. A murderer.

Pilate. Then I delivered unto them the other, that they might crucify him, and saw how he went out to the so-called Place of the Skull (in Hebrew called Golgotha)——

DON JUAN *approaches* L'INCONNUE *and kisses her hand.*

Don Juan. Mademoiselle de la Seine?

L'Inconnue. Who does me this honor?

Don Juan. A man who envies you! Not for the greatness of your fame, which, I fear, is inferior to mine. I envy you, Mademoiselle de la Seine, for the *manner* of your fame!

L'Inconnue. How do you mean that, Monsieur?

Don Juan. All the world imagines that it knows me. All wrong, Mademoiselle, all wrong! The world, on the other hand, admits that it knows nothing of you, nothing but the name: L'Inconnue de la Seine! How I envy you!

L'Inconnue. But I am tubercular—and pregnant. . . .

Don Juan. My name is Don Juan.

The Contemporary. Of Seville? Don Juan Tenorio?

Don Juan. You are mistaken! You know me from the theater. [*To the audience.*] I come from the hell of literature. What things have been imputed to me! Once, after a night of revelry, it's true, I took a short-cut through the cemetery and stumbled over a skull. And I had to laugh, God knows why. I am young, I hate death, that's all. When have I blasphemed against God? The confessor of adulteries in Seville, a priest, Gabriel Tellez, put it into verse. I know. May God punish him for his poetical fantasies! Once there was a beggar, that's true, and I swore at him, for I am a Tenorio, son of a banker, and the alms-giving of the Tenorios disgusts me. But what else do Brecht and his crowd know about me? In the bordello, of which I have no need, I go and play chess. I am considered an intellectual! The love of geometry! Whatever I do or don't do, though, it's all misunderstood and poeticized. Who can put up with that? I am young and I simply want to be what I am. Where is there a land without literature? That's what I'm seeking, ladies and gentlemen: Paradise. I'm seeking the virgin land! [*He turns to* COLUMBUS.] You are, I understand, the discoverer of America?

Columbus. So they call it.

Don Juan. We are compatriots!

Columbus. I am in the service of the Spanish Crown, although born a Genovese——

Don Juan. Honored friend and compatriot, I want to discuss with you the following——

Columbus. It's a question of truth, that's all. We didn't voyage in the name of the Spanish Crown to discover a piece of land which nowadays is called (I don't see why) *America!* To root out and destroy a whole race of people in the name of the Spanish Crown (as later happened)—this we did not voyage for! And that the fields should be torn up in the search for gold: That was not our purpose!

Don Juan. I know, I know.

Columbus. Five years I had to wait, talking and waiting, five years until they built the ships. I said, we will reach India. And then the storm! It was not a question of India, the treasures of India—it was a question of truth! Death and danger and hunger and thirst, God knows, these we endured, and then those nights that I stood chained and fettered to the mast; all those howling nights—I knew that we'd reach India! And we *did* reach India! Why does he shake his head?

Don Juan. I?

Columbus. Him, over there.

Pilate. Yes, yes, what is truth?

Don Juan. I forgot to introduce you: Pontius Pilate. This is the situation, Captain—I want to leave Europe——

L'Inconnue. Ah!

Don Juan. I know, Mademoiselle, what you're thinking now. All honor to Mozart! but it has nothing to do with women. [*He turns to the men.*] Gentlemen, Europe is Death. . . .

SCENE 2

DON JUAN *cannot go on speaking, since their attention is now distracted by a Chinese steward who bows to them ceremoniously.*

DA HING YEN. My name is Da Hing Yen, Master of the Autumn Revels. I have the undeserved honor of announcing to our guests the bill of fare in honor of our victorious generalissimo, Tsin She Hwang Ti, our Great Exalted Emperor, called the Son of Heaven, he who is always in the right and therefore has taken possession of the world.

Pilate. Who?

Da Hing Yen. Tsin She Hwang Ti.

Pilate. Never heard of him.

The Contemporary. Two thousand years before Christ: unknown in Rome; builder of the Chinese Wall.

Da Hing Yen. First course: Soup of young tender bamboo sprouts, horse-radish sprinkled with dew from morning roses, fattened duck liver with rice wine, pheasant à la Peking, pomegranates in Siamese vinegar, stewed swallows' nests——

Don Juan. Stewed?

Da Hing Yen. Stewed. . . . Second course: Tibetan chicken stuffed with young apes' brains, butterfly salad with Indian cherries, broiled pigeons' eggs——

L'Inconnue. Broiled?

Da Hing Yen. Broiled.

L'Inconnue. Go on!

Da Hing Yen. Third course: Assorted fish, caught in the hours of dawn by the imperial cormorants, brought to Nanking by the imperial dispatch riders, garnished with sugared lotus pips, peppered oranges, mussels with sour ant eggs——

SCENE 3

Church music; a black-clad monarch appears.

THE CONTEMPORARY. Sire!

Philip. Knowest thou with whom thou speakst?

The Contemporary. Philip of Spain presumably.

Philip. Why dost thou not kneel?

The Contemporary. Sire—it is urgent——

Philip. Why dost thou not kneel? [THE CONTEMPORARY *kneels down.*] Thou wouldst speak with me?

The Contemporary. Sire—I am—I must confess, Sire—I am really not prepared to clothe in words a subject which I as a citizen of this world have thought much about, especially since —I am not sure, Sire, if you have been informed about developments? We have, to put it briefly, Sire, the Second World War behind us, and now, concerning proud Spain—I wonder, Sire, if I might rise?

Philip. Speak!

The Contemporary. We pay homage to Picasso, García Lorca, Casals——

Philip. Thou hast yet more to say to me.

The Contemporary. I hope you know that the Netherlands are free. Gibraltar is British. Spain has not become a democracy, but rather a foothold for America. And so forth! I will not disturb you, Sire, if you really prefer not.

Philip. The Netherlands—thou darest to say—!

The Contemporary. What the facts are.

Philip. Is there, then, no longer an Inquisition?

The Contemporary. Not *exactly.*

Philip. I have done my duty.

The Contemporary. For that, may God forgive you.

Philip. I know heretics. I burned them by the thousands and the ten thousands. There is no other way.

The Contemporary. You are wrong, Sire. There is another way. Today we have the hydrogen bomb.

Philip. What does that mean?

The Contemporary. That means that the others have it also. And that is the good of it, by your leave, for he who wants to burn up others because they believe differently than he must now burn up himself. It is no longer so simple, Sire, not so simple—to save Christianity! There only remains to us, in fact, the obligation to behave like Christians.

Philip. Mad dreamer!

The Contemporary. Sire——[PHILIP *stands motionless with folded hands.*] In a word: You shall not return, Sire. Remain in the Escorial! There stands your bed, with a peephole before the high altar.

Philip. Thou wast in my sleeping quarters?

The Contemporary. As a tourist. . . . [*He turns to those standing about.*] All of you, my lords, all of you, you must not return. It is too dangerous. Your victories, your kingdoms, your thrones by divine right, your crusades hither and thither, they just don't make sense any more. We want to live. Your way of making history—we can't put up with it any longer. It would be the end, a chain reacton of madness——

A WAITER *appears offering aperitifs.*

Waiter. With or without gin? With or without gin?

The Contemporary. I beg you, gentlemen, to listen to me——

Waiter. With or without gin?

Don Juan. With.

The Contemporary. Sire!—[*He falls to his knees.*] Give us the four freedoms!

Philip. Four—?

The Contemporary. First, the freedom of thought——

Waiter. With or without gin?

THE CONTEMPORARY, *interrupted by the* WAITER, *cannot continue; he kneels, speechless, for a moment before the gently urgent politeness of the* WAITER, *who bows before him, lowering his tray a little.*

Waiter. With or without gin?

SCENE 4

A fanfare. Sound of jubilant voices in the distance.

DA HING YEN. Entry of our Great Exalted Emperor, called the Son of Heaven, into Nanking. . . . Do not miss the opportunity, my lords, of being eyewitnesses to this indescribable spectacle. An unparalleled kaleidoscope of color, gentlemen, a never-before-equaled crowd of people, all throwing themselves on their knees while forty thousand streaming pennants fill the streets of Nanking. An ear-splitting wave of joy, gentlemen, rolls on before our Emperor, who is not yet to be seen. [*Fanfare again.*] Do not miss the opportunity, my lords, of being eyewitnesses to this historic spectacle: The entry of Tsin She Hwang Ti, called the Son of Heaven, into Nanking—which is to say, into the Center of the World. [DA HING YEN *motions toward the right, and* THE MASQUERADERS, *aperitifs in their hands, move toward the right in order to observe the goings-on to best advantage. Only* THE CONTEMPORARY, *who has arisen and dusted off his trousers, hangs back.*] Who are you? Where do you come from? Who invited you? Are you a historical figure?

The Contemporary. Don't trouble yourself.

Da Hing Yen. At any moment the Great Exalted Emperor will appear——

The Contemporary. Tsin She Hwang Ti—or however you pronounce it—the builder of the Chinese Wall. I know. I want to speak to him. [*He lights a cigarette.*] Just think, my friend, today the remains of your wall still stand; every school child has seen pictures of it. And if humanity is destroyed—as seems more likely day by day—along with all these evil spirits who promenade about there and lie in wait for their historical return, deaf and blind to the evolutions of our consciousness—of all the works of man, your wall will be the only thing visible, say, from Mars—this serpent of stone, this monstrosity, this monument of madness, capable of being blown away like the ashes from a cigarette—so—dust of the centuries!

Da Hing Yen. I am Da Hing Yen, Master of the Autumn Revels. If I do not know who someone is, that means: To the Mongolian dogs with him! If I do not understand what someone says, that means: To the Mongolian dogs with him! If I understand that which is not pleasing to our ears, that means——

The Contemporary. Who is that?

Da Hing Yen. Ssh!

DA HING YEN *kowtows and* THE CONTEMPORARY *steps back so as not to be seen.*

SCENE 5

MEE LAN, *the young princess, enters, followed by her maid.*

DA HING YEN. Princess, called Mee Lan, which means Beautiful Orchid! God is gracious to thy simple servant who has the unmerited honor of announcing to you that which will bring sweet joy into the heart of our Princess: The barbarian hounds from the steppes are smashed, the victory is ours, the world is ours!

Mee Lan. What else is new?

Da Hing Yen. Heil. Heil. Heil. [*He backs out kowtowing.*

Mee Lan. What else is new?

Siu. Yesterday, they say, our court jester died.

Mee Lan. Who do you think will take over his job? [*She sits.*] Bring the tea. [*She fans herself.*] What a world! I don't understand them, Siu, they're always talking about victory. I find men so boring. And so stupid. Papa, for example! Now he's sending his drummers all through the empire and he wants to arrest the voice of the people. How can he do *that?*

Siu. Not the voice of the people, Princess. You misunderstood me. They are looking for a man, Min Ko, who *calls* himself "The Voice of the People."

Mee Lan. One man?

Siu. So they say, Princess.

Mee Lan. What kind of man is he?

Siu. Oh, a bad man, they say, a liar, an unbeliever, a destroyer —a very bad man.

Mee Lan. What does he look like?

Siu. That, Princess, no one knows. Only his words are known. They are bad words, they say, lying, unfaithful, destructive, wicked words.

Mee Lan. And as a result Papa wants to kill him?

Siu. Nothing is sacred to him, they say, not even war.

Mee Lan. Ah.

Siu. Therefore they say: His head on the block!

Mee Lan. I am curious. So often I like what Papa considers bad! I'd like to see him!

Siu. Min Ko?

Mee Lan. Papa is comical. He always wants to forbid me whatever is displeasing to him. And the books he forbids me entice me most of all! He is called Min Ko?

Siu. Yes.

Mee Lan. Perhaps it is he?

Siu. Who?

Mee Lan. I want to see him!

Siu. Min Ko?

Mee Lan. Perhaps he is the man I love——

Siu. Princess!

Mee Lan. I love someone, somewhere——[Mee Lan *has risen, fanning herself*.] What else is new? [*She sits again*.]

Siu. Perhaps, Mee Lan, the Prince will also return, the young hero who has been courting you, who won the battle of Liau-tung for love of you. Nothing has yet been heard of his death.

Mee Lan. Nothing yet?

Siu. Mee Lan——

Mee Lan. I don't love him.

Siu. This is the eighth prince, Mee Lan, the eighth!

Mee Lan. I haven't kept count.

Siu. One after another you have sent them into battle because you cannot love them——

Mee Lan. Love!

Siu. The gods will punish you.

Mee Lan. With a handsome head leaning on my breast, do you mean? And suddenly they get all fishy-eyed. And their hands get like slippery fins. Ugh! I have to laugh every time they try, these princes, and then they become angry and leap onto their horses and plunder some province somewhere so that I will take them seriously: If *that's* love—!

Siu. You are pledged to the Prince, Mee Lan, if he survives the war.

Mee Lan. And above all, this stupid blood pounding in my ears? I don't like that—no! Everything is so—so inexpressibly ——[MEE LAN *breaks her fan.*] I won't put up with it! [*She rises.*] Bring us the tea! And inquire if it is true that nothing has yet been heard of the Prince's death.

[SIU *kowtows and exits.*

SCENE 6

MEE LAN. You look at me and are silent. The eighth prince! I don't deny I hope he never returns. But what have I done that you are so silent? He will die for me—all of them say that. Then let them do it! I know, you find me common and base. You feel that a true Chinese girl should not speak like this, a daughter of the Great Exalted Emperor, called the Son of Heaven, a princess in silk and jade, whose duty it is to wait for a prince——[*She protests.*] I am not a Chinese girl! [*She looks at the spectators.*] You think you can prescribe my duty to me? You think I don't know that I am disguised, in costume? And you, who are grown up and know everything, do you really believe, for example, that Papa is always in the right? I am not stupid. You think I don't know that everything here (for example, this throne—even a schoolgirl can see it) everything here is nothing but theater? But you sit and look at one another. You, who are grown up and wise, you sit, your arms folded over your breast, and you are silent—and no one comes forward and says what it really is, and no one dares and is a man!

SCENE 7

THE CONTEMPORARY *steps forward from his hiding place.*

THE CONTEMPORARY. Miss——[MEE LAN *sees him and screams.*] Don't be afraid.

Mee Lan. Help! Siu! Help! Siu, Siu——

The Contemporary. I haven't been spying on you. Please.

Mee Lan. Who are you?

The Contemporary. Calm yourself. I'm sorry if I frightened you. Don't be afraid of me. I'm no prince.

Mee Lan. Who are you?

The Contemporary. I want to speak with the Emperor of China. Why do you stare at me like that? This is the costume of our time; business suit, ready-made.

Mee Lan. Who are you?

The Contemporary. Shall we sit down?

He leads her toward the chairs in the foreground.

Mee Lan. Are you—Min Ko?

The Contemporary. Me? But why?

Mee Lan. And you have dared to enter the imperial park—— [*She falls silent with astonishment, then gestures toward the other chair.*]

The Contemporary. Thank you very much! [*He sits down and crosses his legs.*] An elegant park! Your papa, the Great Exalted Emperor, will be coming in at any moment, I believe. How old are you?

Mee Lan. Seventeen.

The Contemporary. I really didn't mean to spy on you.

Mee Lan. But where have you come from so suddenly?

The Contemporary. I—er—how shall I put it—? [*He takes a cigarette.*] I come from another time. I am older than you, Princess, by some two thousand years.

Mee Lan. Then do you know our future?

The Contemporary. In a certain sense, oh, yes. That which concerns the future of this empire, for example——

Mee Lan. And mine? Mine? Speak! Whom will I marry? I can't stand this prince. But who else is coming toward me in my future? I sit and wait—you can see—in hope and fear, with open eyes, yet blind, for not an hour can I see forward, not even a minute! And you know the future two thousand years from now? [*He snaps on his cigarette lighter.*] Oh, tell me what you know!

SIU, *the maid, brings tea. Silence. Soft music is heard in the distance.* SIU *kowtows and disappears.*

The Contemporary. What we know?

Mee Lan. Speak!

The Contemporary. Item: Energy equals mass times the speed of light squared. Whereby the speed of light (one hundred eighty-six thousand miles a second) is the single absolute power with which we are able to reckon nowadays. Everything else, we know, is relative.

Mee Lan. I don't understand that.

The Contemporary. Item: Even time is relative. Seat yourself on a ray of light, Princess, and you will become convinced: There is (for you) no space, therefore likewise no time. And your every thought will be endlessly slow. "No!" you think, "I don't want to be eternal!" and you dismount from your ray of light. And you will return here (I swear it to you) not a second older. On our earth, however, there have been—look—two thousand years in the meantime——

Mee Lan. Two thousand years?

The Contemporary. Irredeemably.

Mee Lan. And I?

The Contemporary. You, Princess, live on—today.

Mee Lan. How do you sit on a ray of light?

The Contemporary. Time is a function of space. That, for example, is what we know. And there is actually neither time nor space! Nor truth, for we are so created that we can exist only in time and space. . . . You are seventeen?

Mee Lan. Yes.

The Contemporary. I am thirty-four, twice as old as you, Princess. An impossible pair!

Mee Lan. Why?

The Contemporary. Do you see that reddish star?

Mee Lan. Which one?

The Contemporary. There, above my thumb! [*They gaze up, heads close together.*] See it?

Mee Lan. Yes.

The Contemporary. Suppose I emigrate to that reddish star, whizzing along at an ungodly speed (let's say, one hundred fifty thousand miles per second) and you, Princess, remain here——

Mee Lan. I remain here?

The Contemporary. And now let's compare our ages. I will leave you my wrist watch. And look, you will be convinced: We are both seventeen!

Mee Lan. Really?

The Contemporary. Suppose I am whizzing toward that reddish star and then, to be sure, we are the same age, according to your earth time. But also, Princess, I am adjusting our ages and measuring according to my then-and-there time, and behold: you are seventeen while I am almost sixty, a graybeard, no longer worthy your falling in love with.

Mee Lan. Ah!

The Contemporary. So what happens now?

Mee Lan. Tell me!

The Contemporary. Nothing to either of us, Princess, or something to both of us, but later, not now, where we are. On this earth, as I said, we are seventeen and thirty-four. But *tempus absolutum,* a universal time such as man hitherto believed in, a time that embraces all and everything—no, there is no such thing.

Mee Lan. That is what you know!?

The Contemporary. Among other things.

Mee Lan. And what do you know about men?

The Contemporary. That they measure wrong, always, in space that is not endless, yet is unlimited—space that curves back in upon itself at its borders.

Mee Lan. Ah.

The Contemporary. Read Einstein.

Mee Lan. I can't picture it.

The Contemporary. No one, Princess, not even a contemporary, can picture it, any more than he can picture God.

Mee Lan. You believe in a God?

The Contemporary. What shall I say to that? Energy equals mass times the speed of light squared, which means: mass is energy, an ungodly ball of energy. And woe to the world if it goes wrong! And it *does* go wrong. It's been doing it presumably for two million years. What is our sun? An explosion. All the cosmos: one giant explosion. It's flying apart. And what will remain? The greater probability—so our modern physics teaches us—is that it will be chaos, the collapse of the mass. Creation—so our modern physics teaches us—was a vast improbability.

Energy will remain, with no loss, with no possibility. Destruction by heat of the world! That is the end: unalterable endlessness, nothingness.

Mee Lan. I asked if you believe in a God.

The Contemporary. Man discovered the microscope. But the deeper he was able to penetrate into creation, the less was there any creator to be seen. In order to compensate for the loss of God, man established the law of cause and effect. We considered everything else to be wrong. But suddenly behold: an atom with suicidal free will: the radium atom. And then the behavior of the electrons! And matter, the only thing we can count on, what is it? A dance of numbers, a ghostly diagram. So today we have come this far: God, who could not be found in the microscope, still calls us menacingly to the inevitable reckoning. Anyone who does not think of Him has ceased to think. Why are you looking at me like that?

Mee Lan. I don't know. . . .

The Contemporary. What don't you know?

Mee Lan. If you are the one whom I have awaited. . . .

The Contemporary. Awaited? Me?

Mee Lan. Oh, say that you are!

DA HING YEN, *the Master of the Revels, comes in with three soldiers.*

Da Hing Yen. There he is. To the Mongolian dogs with him!

The soldiers obey, throw a noose over THE CONTEMPORARY, *but* MEE LAN *jumps up, removes the noose, and places it around the neck of the Master of the Revels.*

Mee Lan. To the Mongolian dogs with him!

The soldiers obey and haul out DA HING YEN *howling fearfully.*

The Contemporary. Thanks.

Mee Lan. Do you drink tea?

The Contemporary. As I said, I have come to talk to the Emperor of China. For in view of all that we now know it's clear that things cannot go on like this. The calculations of our learned men have been proved correct: unfortunately, quite fatally correct. I don't know, Princess, if you have heard of the hydrogen bomb——

Mee Lan. Is that what you want to talk to Papa about?

The Contemporary. It's a question of whether or not the rulers of the world understand that things can't go on like this. Others are of the opinion that the rulers of the world should not be persuaded reasonably, but simply hanged. Only I'm afraid that even the revolution which stands this moment before your gates is too late——[MEE LAN *offers him a cup.*] Oh—thank you, Princess, thank you very much! [*He takes the cup and holds it.*] By the way—what gave you the idea that I was Min Ko?

Mee Lan. Papa wants to kill him. His head on the block! Papa is looking for him throughout the whole empire. If you are he——

The Contemporary. Min Ko. That means "The Voice of the People"?

Mee Lan. Yes.

The Contemporary. I am an intellectual. [*He drinks tea.*] Delicious tea! Oh, yes, we have often thought, over and over, that one of us, an intellectual, might be "The Voice of the People," beginning with Kung Fu Tse, your teacher.

Mee Lan. You know Kung Fu Tse?

The Contemporary. "Every man among the people earns his title according to what he can do. He enjoys the fruits of his labor in his time. He takes his position according to his labors. In this fashion, true brotherhood will be achieved. When the people live in brotherhood, then dissatisfaction will be rare and discord will not arise. This is the basis upon which state and home will build and long endure."

Mee Lan. Kung Fu Tse said that?

The Contemporary. Kung Fu Tse said that. I wonder: Was Kung Fu Tse "The Voice of the People!"?

DA HING YEN II, *the successor to his unfortunate predecessor of the same name, enters with the same three soldiers.*

Da Hing Yen II. My name is Da Hing Yen, Master of the Autumn Revels. If I don't know who someone is, that means: To the Mongolian dogs with him! If I do not understand what someone says, that means: To the Mongolian dogs with him! If I understand that which is not pleasing to our ears, that means: To the Mongolian dogs with him!

The soldiers obey, and everything is repeated: they put the noose over THE CONTEMPORARY, *but* MEE LAN *jumps up, takes it off and throws it over the neck of the Master of the Revels.*

Mee Lan. To the Mongolian dogs with him!

The soldiers obey and DA HING YEN II *is dragged out howling even more fearfully than the first one.*

The Contemporary. Do you have any more of these?

Mee Lan. It's a much sought-after job. [*They take up their cups again.*] You were speaking of Kung Fu Tse. . . .

They look at one another.

The Contemporary. You are a lovely girl. [MEE LAN *drops her cup.*] What is it, Mee Lan? You're crying?

MEE LAN *jumps up and turns away.*

Mee Lan. No! I won't have it. No! And this stupid blood pounding in my ears. No! That everything is so—so inexpressibly——

The Contemporary. Mee Lan! Your name is still Mee Lan?

Mee Lan. Don't touch me!

The Contemporary. You're all mixed up. What's happened? You're confused, Princess; think of the two thousand years between us. . . .

Mee Lan. I love you in spite of them.

The Contemporary. But seriously . . .

Mee Lan. I love you in spite of them.

The Contemporary. Mee Lan . . . ?

Mee Lan. I love you.

She kisses him. And then he kisses her. DA HING YEN III *enters, kowtows.* MEE LAN *and* THE CONTEMPORARY *remain in an embrace.*

Da Hing Yen. My name is Da Hing Yen, Master of the Autumn Revels. God is gracious to thy simple servant who has the unmerited honor of announcing that which will bring joy into the heart of the Princess: Your father, Tsin She Hwang Ti, is here! [*Drum roll.*] Heil. Heil. Heil.

[DA HING YEN *disappears.*

Mee Lan. What will I do when you are not beside me? Kiss the stones, embrace the pillars, kiss the leaves of the trees; oh, I will walk in the river embracing wave upon wave, I will talk with dogs and with clouds, and when I walk in the sun I will close my eyes in order to feel your warmth. I will go mad without you. And when I cannot sleep, the night winds will caress me, and if you do not come, I will be sick until I find you. . . . You are silent?

The Contemporary. You are speaking.

Mee Lan. Is it true? I don't know. Where did you get this scar? I feel you like a blind person. From a serpent's bite? No, it was in a child's game with bow and arrow.

The Contemporary. An accident.

Mee Lan. I want to know everything about you!

The Contemporary. Your father was just announced.

Mee Lan. Here in your arms like this I could hear them say over me: Tomorrow you will die, struck down by lightning, and your grave will be prepared! and I would not tremble, it would not touch me, if I could only feel myself in your arms!

The Contemporary. Mee Lan——

Mee Lan. How I have planned and dreamed: You would be thus and so and such and such! And now you are simply what you are, and I am glad.

The Contemporary. Don't you hear me?

Mee Lan. Don't tell me there's another woman!

The Contemporary. Your father was just announced.

Mee Lan. There *is* another woman?

The Contemporary. I want to tell you how it is——

Fanfare.

Mee Lan. Hide yourself! They're coming! And wait for me!

The Contemporary. And you?

Mee Lan. I will come—to your time!

SCENE 8

Deployment of EUNUCHS *in preparation for the reception of the Emperor.*

DA HING YEN. Line up on both sides, as I ordered! And here, where is the interval? Thirteen paces for eunuchs!

Journalist. Excuse me, but we're not the eunuchs, we're the gentlemen of the press!

Da Hing Yen. Thirteen paces, I said! [*A flash bulb explodes.*] *What—was—that?!*

Journalist. Thank you!

Fanfare for the second time, and the EUNUCHS *prostrate themselves. However, instead of the Emperor, two promenading masqueraders appear:* L'INCONNUE DE LA SEINE *and a man in a toga. They pause on the steps.*

The Toga. I said to myself:
"It must be by his death; and for my part,
I known no personal cause to spurn at him
But for the general; he would be crowned."

DA HING YEN *gestures that they should disappear.*

The Toga. I said to myself:
"It is the bright day that brings forth the adder,
And that craves wary walking. Crown him? That—
And then, I grant, we put a sting in him
That at his will he may do danger with."

DA HING YEN *gestures that they should disappear.*

The Toga. "And therefore think him as a serpent's egg

Which, hatched, would, as his kind, grow mischievous,
And kill him in the shell."

L'INCONNUE *takes his arm.*

L'Inconnue. We mustn't pass through here.

The Toga. What do you mean?

L'Inconnue. Something is going on here, it seems.

The Toga. I don't like these ceremonies.

L'Inconnue. It doesn't concern us, my noble friend. They are honoring their emperor, that's all.

The Toga. But I thought Caesar was dead!

Fanfare for the third time, and TSIN SHE HWANG TI, *Emperor of China, appears on the steps. He has a round, soft face, a gentle voice. He is smiling. He is absolutely the opposite of the bloodthirsty tyrant we have expected. He seems almost timid.*

Hwang Ti. My loyal subjects!

The Eunuchs. Heil! Heil! Heil!

THE TOGA *steps forward toward the* EUNUCHS.

Brutus. My name is Brutus, whoever you may be.
(It's like an evil dream; the icy sweat
Runs on my forehead as I look at you,
There where you kneel and huzzah and exult
As though what we have done was done in vain.)
Listen to Brutus! I with my own hand
Struck down the mighty Caesar, he who was
My friend, until, ambitious, deaf to friends,
Who offered their advice, their pleas, their warning,
He lay before us, dead, a fallen tyrant.
And what has happened since? Do you permit
That bold and shameless tyranny should thrive
Till all free will and action disappear?
Now is the time; do not delude yourselves;

You have, unquestioned by your judgments,
Robbed yourselves of all your dearest rights;
And for the common good to fight you have
(How long?) a single weapon, friends—a dagger!

L'Inconnue. Come on! We're only interrupting!

Brutus. Shall Rome (the world) quake before one man?

L'Inconnue. It's no use, my noble friend. They don't hear you. All that happened in a completely different time.

Brutus. Is Caesar then not dead? And has not Brutus
Atoned for his friend's blood upon this dagger
With his dear wife's and his own poor life?
Is this what history means, that men's mistakes
Keep returning endlessly forever?

L'Inconnue. Come!

Brutus. It's like an evil dream, whene'er I see . . .

L'Inconnue. Let's go to the pond, my noble friend, I will show you the goldfish.

She takes BRUTUS *away.*

Hwang Ti. My loyal subjects! Since I have been upon this throne, as you well know, I have fought for only one thing: Peace—but not for a barbarous peace, rather for a true peace, a conclusive peace, which is to say—for the Great Order, which we call the True Order and the Happy Order and the Final Order.

The Eunuchs. Heil! Heil! Heil!

Hwang Ti. My loyal subjects! It is achieved: The world is free. That is all that I can say to you at this moment: The world is free. I stand before you with a full heart. The barbarian hordes of the steppes are silenced, they who opposed the Great Peace—as you know, they wanted a twenty-year peace treaty!—and the world is ours, which is to say: there is now in the world only one Order, our Order, which we call the Great Order and the True Order and the Final Order.

The Eunuchs. Heil! Heil! Heil!

Hwang Ti. Here is my plan—[*He takes out a parchment scroll.*] Do not fear the future, my loyal subjects. For, as things are now, so they will remain. We will forestall any future. [*He gives the scroll to* DA HING YEN.] Read!

DA HING YEN *kowtows, then reads.*

Da Hing Yen. "The Chinese Wall, or the Great Wall. In Chinese: Wan-li-chang-cheng; literally, the Ten Thousand Li Wall. The greatest structure in the world. Up to sixteen meters high and (defensively) over five meters wide. It begins west of Suchou and ends at the Gulf of Liautung. Built as defense against the northwestern barbarian hordes under Tsin She Hwang Ti (221-210 B.C.)."

Hwang Ti. It will be started tomorrow.

The Eunuchs. Heil. Heil. Heil.

Hwang Ti. What remains for preparation for the ceremonies is, I hope, in readiness; our guests are all assembled?

Da Hing Yen. A slight oversight, Your Majesty. A gentleman named Hitler, apparently a German, is not to be admitted. My predecessors didn't trust him, since this gentleman made such a terrible impression at first glance, and my unfortunate predecessors felt that, generally speaking, Germans don't look like that.

Hwang Ti. Hm.

Da Hing Yen. The gentlemen from Moscow adhere to their "nyet."

Hwang Ti. And the ladies?

Da Hing Yen. A youthful Queen of Egypt, Your Majesty, who is complaining that she has nothing to wear—literally nothing. She protests that this is historically accurate.

Hwang Ti. Lest we forget: Before we proceed to the great banquet in order to enjoy ourselves, and so that your joy, my loyal subjects, shall be complete, one more word—there now remains but one last enemy, a single adversary in our empire, one man who calls himself "The Voice of the People." You know him as Min Ko. You know his sayings. With abhorrence, I know, with abhorrence. Well, you can take comfort now. Min Ko has been captured.

Mee Lan. Min Ko?

Hwang Ti. I am going to bring him to trial.

Da Hing Yen. Before we dine?

Hwang Ti. It won't take us long. You, however, my loyal subjects, prepare for the feast. It will be the feast of our lives. Let there be music, classical music. Let there be nothing lacking for the delight of ourselves and our foreign guests. Let there be incense and theater, cost what it may, fireworks and culture!

Gong. DA HING YEN *and the others withdraw.*

SCENE 9

HWANG TI *and* MEE LAN *are alone.*

HWANG TI. Greetings, my child, you above all!

Mee Lan. Papa . . .

Hwang Ti. Mee Lan: my lovely orchid! [*He seats himself on the throne and relaxes.*] It is achieved. At last I can say it! A final adversary, a single one—I laugh at him, at all who hope to change the future. They will not survive their future. For power is ours. And we who have that power, we need no future. For we are happy. I will forestall the future. I will build a wall —that is, the people will build it—— My child, why are you looking at me like that?

Mee Lan. I don't know, Papa, how much you know.

Hwang Ti. About what?

Mee Lan. About the future. . . . I can't explain it. But, if I understand it rightly, our future, Papa, lies behind us. We are (if I understand it rightly) two thousand years behind reality. And it's all untrue. I don't know, Papa, whether you know it or not.

Hwang Ti. What is untrue?

Mee Lan. The show that's being played here. All. Your whole empire. Nothing but theater. . . .

HWANG TI *gives a fatherly chuckle.*

Hwang Ti. You have read too much, my child. You talk all this intellectual nonsense, my child, and you know I don't like that sort of thing. The Atomic Age! You read that in all the newspapers. Sit by me and be a child, as you ought to be: a happy child, a nice child, a positive child. Sit down! For I have, my child, good tidings for you. [MEE LAN *sits on the steps.*] He is alive!

Mee Lan. Who?

Hwang Ti. Your prince, Wu Tsiang—Prince Charming! The Brave Prince, who has earned that title in action. It hung in the balance—unforeseen, they swooped down from the north and the south, the barbarian dogs of the steppes! We were surrounded!—that is to say, not us, of course, but our troops. Do you understand, my child, what that meant? Then up spoke Wu Tsiang the Brave: "We will fight to the last man!" And so it happened. He sacrificed his entire army, thirty thousand men——

Mee Lan. And he himself survived?

Hwang Ti. He is a born general, no doubt about it! His fatherland owes him its praise. And now within the hour he will appear, my child, as your suitor before the assembled court. [MEE LAN *jumps up violently.*] What is it? [MEE LAN *fans herself furiously, back to her father, silent.*] What does this mean?

Mee Lan. What you already know, Papa: I will marry no prince.

Hwang Ti. My dear child——

Mee Lan. It's out of the question.

Hwang Ti. Why?

Mee Lan. I no longer believe in princes.

Hwang Ti. Then whom do you wish to marry?

Mee Lan. Min Ko.

Hwang Ti. What's that you say?

Mee Lan. I will marry Min Ko.

Hwang Ti. A water-carrier?

Mee Lan. Laugh, Papa—I'm laughing too—Min Ko arrested, when no one even knows what he looks like!

Hwang Ti. Now that he *is* arrested, we know very well how he looks—this water-carrier, this gaping fool, this mule-driver. Why do you smile? We paraded through the city and when people saw their emperor, they roared with joy. Only one man, once, did not roar. I saw him immediately. He gaped at me without making a sound. I said to my people: "I wonder what that voiceless one is thinking. Seize him after I have passed!"

Mee Lan. And?

Hwang Ti. All the others, scarcely had I passed but they were roaring with joy——

Mee Lan. Then turned away, I can well imagine, and murmured their mocking words as always.

Hwang Ti. True.

Mee Lan. With the exception of this one.

Hwang Ti. True.

Mee Lan. And so he has been arrested, this lone brave man?

Hwang Ti. Anyone who flaunts his bravery as openly as that, my child, is sure to be a pretty rascal, indeed. I don't like bravery. I don't trust it. Why didn't he roar with joy, eh? Tell me that.

Mee Lan. I don't know. Maybe he is mute.

Hwang Ti. Mute?

Mee Lan. That happens, you know.

Hwang Ti. Mute. Most amusing. We search for Min Ko, The Voice of the People, and now he wants us to believe that we have arrested a mute. What does that mean—that he is making fools of us again?

Mee Lan. Papa . . .

Hwang Ti. Why should he be mute? Why him, of all people?

[Hwang Ti *gets up*.] We'll see about this. We have a way of making him speak.

Mee Lan. You're going to have him tortured—?

Hwang Ti. Until he confesses.

Mee Lan. Torture a mute—?

Hwang Ti. Until he confesses! [*For the first time* Hwang Ti *loses his gentle voice and bellows suddenly*.] It must be *someone!* What's the good of all our victories, the greatness of all our victories, when the mocker goes on with his blasphemies? Am I never, never, to enjoy my peace? We can't win any more great victories; there are no enemies left. Do you grasp what that means? There are no more enemies left——[Hwang Ti, *who has been pacing about in his rage, stops suddenly*.] Who is that?

SCENE 10

THE CONTEMPORARY *steps forward from his place of concealment.*

THE CONTEMPORARY. Allow me to introduce myself——

Hwang Ti. Are you Min Ko? [HWANG TI *draws his dagger.*]

Mee Lan. Papa! [MEE LAN *springs between them.*]

Hwang Ti. Who are you?

The Contemporary. An intellectual.

Hwang Ti. A—what?

The Contemporary. Doctor of Jurisprudence.

Hwang Ti. You come most appropriately, Doctor of Jurisprudence! [*He replaces his dagger.*] Go and call the mandarins of my court to assemble. Bring in the water-carrier whom we have arrested. I will hold trial—here and now.

The Contemporary. Your Majesty——

Hwang Ti. Why don't you go?

The Contemporary. I wanted to speak with you, Your Majesty.

Hwang Ti. What?

The Contemporary. My knowledge of history is not particularly extensive, and yet perhaps of some use to you.

Hwang Ti. Do you know the future?

The Contemporary. If you leave out of account certain modern scientific accomplishments—then yes, Your Majesty, generally.

Hwang Ti. We are going to build a wall——

The Contemporary. Against the barbarians: I know. For the barbarians are always the others. That's still true today, Your Majesty. And culture, that's always us. And therefore we must liberate other people, for we (and not the others) are the Free World.

Hwang Ti. Do you doubt it?

The Contemporary. I have just seen your naked dagger, Your Majesty. How can I doubt it?

Hwang Ti. What do you mean by that?

The Contemporary. That I want to live.

Hwang Ti. And why don't you do what I order?

The Contemporary. Did you order me to speak the truth (insofar as we understand it) or did you order me to call the people to a Donkey Court?

Hwang Ti. Donkey Court?

The Contemporary. I'm only asking. [HWANG TI *draws his dagger again.*] Your Majesty—I understand!

[THE CONTEMPORARY *kowtows and goes.*

Hwang Ti. But he didn't dare, you notice, he didn't dare! [MEE LAN *follows* THE CONTEMPORY.] Mee Lan? Mee Lan!

SCENE 11

HWANG TI, *left suddenly alone, turns toward the audience.*

HWANG TI. I know well enough what you're thinking, you out there. But I laugh at your hopes. You're thinking, this very evening you will see me hurled from this throne, for the play must have an ending and a moral, and when I am dethroned then you can complacently return home and drink your beer and nibble on a cracker. That's what you would like. You with your dramaturgy! I laugh. Go out and buy your evening newspaper, you out there, and on the first page you will find my name. For I do not intend to be dethroned. I don't believe in dramaturgy.

SCENE 12

A young Egyptian princess, attractively unclad, now appears.

CLEOPATRA. I find you alone, my lord, and not in the serene good humor appropriate for such a masquerade party.

Hwang Ti. Who are you?

Cleopatra. How can you ask? I am Cleopatra. Or have I disguised myself too thoroughly? [*She sits on his knee.*] Why so grave?

Hwang Ti. The situation is grave.

Cleopatra. Oh, well, hasn't it been for centuries?

Hwang Ti. Never as grave as it is today.

Cleopatra. I remember, that's what Caesar said, too—and also Antony. I understand you great men who make history. Sometimes you are Roman, sometimes Spanish, sometimes Chinese. Only I, you notice, never change costumes. I love all men who make history. Indeed, I love all *men*—[*She caresses* HWANG TI.] How lonely you must be!

Hwang Ti. Since I have been on this throne, I have fought for one cause and one cause only: Peace! By which I mean, of course: for the Great Order, which we call the True Order and the Only Order and the Final Order! For thirteen years I have said, again and again and again, that I am their Savior. Why won't they believe me? For thirteen years they have gone around slandering me, and then, if I have one of these slanderers killed, I am considered a murderer.

Cleopatra. Really?

Hwang Ti. Am I a bloodsucker?

Cleopatra. Who says that?

Hwang Ti. Min Ko.

Cleopatra. Kill him! [*She caresses him.*]

Hwang Ti. They drive me to it, you know. For thirteen years they've been driving me to it. For thirteen years they've been saying: There's no such thing as a government that's always right. And so for thirteen years they've driven me from victory to victory. Do they think I make war because I *like* to? They don't want me to have any peace.

Cleopatra. I understand.

Hwang Ti. But now what? The world is ours, yet no one understands what that means. The situation is now more serious than ever: There are no more victories possible! The world is ours! [CLEOPATRA *strokes him soothingly.*] You say your name is Cleopatra?

Cleopatra. I am the girl who offers consolation to the victors. However I can! I was scarcely a child when Caesar came. He considered himself the Master of the World, and so naturally he moved me to pity. And then Antony! he needed me so desperately in order to enjoy his victories.

Hwang Ti. Cleopatra!

Cleopatra. Yes?

Hwang Ti. Tell me, just once——

Cleopatra. I believe in you!

HWANG TI, *overjoyed by her correct answer, kisses her naked thigh, as* DA HING YEN *appears.*

Hwang Ti. Yes. What is it *now?*

Da Hing Yen. Wu Tsiang, better known as the Brave Prince, wishes to make known his arrival. He has just this moment leaped off the galloping horse which has dropped dead beneath him!

Hwang Ti. Let him approach. [DA HING YEN *withdraws.*] This prince comes as though in answer to my prayers. I will retire from the business of government. What do you think? The Prince is going to marry my daughter and take over the burdens of history. What do I want here on this throne? I am not like this. People misunderstand me.

Cleopatra. I don't.

Hwang Ti. Fundamentally, you see, I am a simple man——

Cleopatra. Make it short and sweet with this prince!

Hwang Ti. I will retire—yes, that's it! That's all I've ever really wanted from the beginning. Somewhere in the country. I adore nature. Fundamentally, I'm an introvert. A little bungalow is all I ask. And I will read a good book, some book I've always wanted to read, perhaps by this Kung Fu Tse, and I will raise bees. Or I will go fishing. That's all I want to be on this earth: a poor, simple fisherman——

Cleopatra. And a landscape painter!

Hwang Ti. How do you know that, my sweet?

Cleopatra. Because, my sweet, I do *not* misunderstand you.

Hwang Ti. Cleopatra!

HWANG TI, *again overjoyed by her answer, again kisses her naked thigh, as* WU TSIANG, *the Prince, appears.*

SCENE 13

THE PRINCE. Long live Hwang Ti, our Great Exalted Emperor, called the Son of Heaven, he who is always in the right, the Savior of the Fatherland—all hail! [*Drum roll.*] All hail! [*Drum roll.*] All hail! [*Drum roll.* HWANG TI *returns the elaborate gestures of greeting.*]

Hwang Ti. You come in good time, Hero of Liautung. He who comes through such a battle as the only survivor of his entire army is an officer of stature, we know, and therefore I repeat: You come in good time, Prince, a time of celebration and gratitude.

The Prince. He who fulfills his duty because it *is* his duty has no need, Your Majesty, either of reward or thanks.

Hwang Ti. We know only too well, my Prince, of your noble disposition, which nevertheless will not hinder us from awarding you the highest order in our realm: for the medals are there, and the more dead there are, the more medals to go around for the survivors.

The Prince. Your Majesty, I have not fought for medals——

Hwang Ti. Not another word!

The Prince. I have fought for Peace, and for that Order which we call the True Order and the Happy Order and the Final Order.

Hwang Ti. We know that, Prince. The gratitude of the Fatherland awaits you. I will keep my word: My child shall be your wife, Hero of Liautung, this very night!

They repeat the complicated ceremony of soldierly greetings, then suddenly change their whole tone and manner; THE

PRINCE *takes off his Chinese helmet, puffs loudly, and mops the sweat from his brow.*

The Prince. Phew!

Cleopatra. I take it you're thirsty?

The Prince. Talk about *hot!*

Cleopatra. Vodka or whiskey—what do they drink hereabouts?

The Prince. These historical costumes are suffocating! I'm all chafed around my neck.

Cleopatra. And you, my lord, what do you drink?

Hwang Ti. We drink no alcoholic beverages.

Cleopatra. Ha! Do-gooder! [CLEOPATRA *mixes drinks.*]

Hwang Ti. Now, to get down to business, my dear Prince: this affair of the Great Wall——

The Prince. Right!

Hwang Ti. You've received my letters?

The Prince. Right!

Hwang Ti. You take over the management. I will, of course, be Chairman of the Board of Directors. And, as noted, we'll stick to the sandstone.

The Prince. I hear that granite would be better.

Hwang Ti. My sandstone is cheaper.

The Prince. Ah.

Hwang Ti. Your father advises us to use granite, I know. Your father is a loyal mandarin, and his province, I hear, is full of granite. Also full of timber. And my provinces, as far as I know, are poor in timber. What I *am* able to sell the Fatherland, however, is sandstone. Thus it has occurred to me: The construction will require lots of scaffolding. Lots of timber, which your worthy father can supply——

The Prince. At what price?

Hwang Ti. Oh, I don't understand prices——

CLEOPATRA *hands* THE PRINCE *a glass.*

The Prince. Thank you very much! [*He starts to drink.*]

Hwang Ti. I have still another concern, Prince——

The Prince. The labor supply?

Hwang Ti. We need a good million men, and many are going to die; nevertheless the figure of a million must remain stable, that's clear. And our people, I hear, are not enthusiastic over the plan.

The Prince. So much the better!

Hwang Ti. How is that?

The Prince. So much the cheaper! Whoever is not enthusiastic over the plan is obviously an enemy, and therefore becomes a slave-laborer. [*He lifts his glass.*] Your health! [*He drinks.* THE CONTEMPORARY *enters.*] Who is this?

Hwang Ti. My new court jester.

The Prince. Ah.

Hwang Ti. My Doctor of Jurisprudence.

SCENE 14

Hwang Ti. What do you want?

The Contemporary. The lords of your court, Your Majesty, are assembled, as ordered, for the Donkey Court. The defendant has been advised that it is useless for him to plead innocent and that things will go more smoothly if he accuses himself of high treason. The death sentence has already been drawn up.

Hwang Ti. Good.

The Contemporary. And that's no joke.

Hwang Ti. You see, my dear Prince, how all things fulfill themselves this day: Min Ko, my last adversary, is in custody——

The Prince. I have heard about that, Your Majesty—in no uncertain terms.

Hwang Ti. Where?

The Prince. I am delighted, Your Majesty, to find you in such good spirits in spite of the uproar before your gates. I couldn't have gotten through that mob without the aid of my trusty followers. They chased us, and when I cried: "Open in the name of the Emperor!" they hooted and threw stones at us. "Hand him over!" they bellowed. "Give us the Emperor!"

Hwang Ti. Before my gates?

The Prince. Nine of my men are dead, not to speak of my horse. We had to carve an alley through the mob with our naked sabers. Look, Your Majesty, see the blood on my boots!

Hwang Ti. Rioting?

The Prince. You didn't know about it?

CLEOPATRA *hands a glass to* HWANG TI.

Cleopatra. That one's for you, my lord.

Hwang Ti. No alcohol?

Cleopatra. Word of honor!

HWANG TI *takes the glass.*

The Prince. Your health!

Hwang Ti. Why should there be rioting?

The Prince. They want to set him free.

Hwang Ti. Min Ko?

The Prince. To keep him from being brought to trial.

Hwang Ti. He will be brought to trial.

The Prince. Anything else would be considered a sign of weakness.

Hwang Ti. His head on the block! [HWANG TI *drinks, leaving himself with a milk mustache.*]

The Contemporary. And if the trial is not just?

Hwang Ti. Be still.

The Contemporary. Right.

Hwang Ti. Was there something you wanted to say?

The Contemporary. Nothing.

Hwang Ti. We need a head, my dear Doctor of Jurisprudence. It *could* be yours. Was there something you wanted to say?

The Contemporary. I just wanted to say—well, for example —er, if you will allow me, Your Majesty—you have milk on your upper lip.

Hwang Ti. You had something else you wanted to say!

The Contemporary. What?

Hwang Ti. Would you like to be The Voice of the People?

The Contemporary. I wanted to say: Nowadays—it's not very common for the people to go marching through the streets. Nowadays, after all, weapons—which the people don't have—keep getting better. Nevertheless, it happens. But nowadays—we don't get excited about these things, Your Majesty, we know as a matter of course: These are not the real people, out there in the streets, those are not *our* people!

The Prince. But rather—?

The Contemporary. Agitators. Spies. Terrorists. Undesirable Elements.

The Prince. And what does that mean?

The Contemporary. That means: The rulers determine who the people are. And those persons who are out there demonstrating in the streets today cannot be expected to be treated like people. For the real people—the *real* people—are always satisfied with their rulers.

Hwang Ti. Good.

The Prince. Very good.

The Contemporary. Isn't it true? The blood on your splendid boots, Prince—how could that be the blood of the people? It would be a painful thought, wouldn't it? Very painful.

Hwang Ti. What were those words again?

The Contemporary. Terrorists, Undesirable Elements, Agitators. Very helpful words, Your Majesty; they nip truth in the bud.

Hwang Ti. Doctor of Jurisprudence, you will remain in our service.

The Contemporary. And this, too, Your Majesty, is no joke.

HWANG TI *rises and repeats the ceremony of salutes.*

Hwang Ti. Hero of Liautung! [THE PRINCE *rises and puts his helmet back on.*] I greet you, Hero of Liautung, as my son-in-law and heir to my kingdom; *if* you are able to pass the final test!

The Prince. Your Majesty.

Hwang Ti. Undesirable Elements are at our gates. . . .

The Prince. I understand.

Hwang Ti. You know what hangs in the balance.

The Prince. I will deal with them as they deserve, as Agitators, Spies, and Terrorists.

Hwang Ti. I have complete confidence in you, Prince. You are loyalty personified. You battle for a kingdom that is sacred to you, my dear Prince, you battle for your own heritage! [The PRINCE *repeats the ceremonial saluting.*] We will meet again later, I hope, in fireworks and festivities!

HWANG TI *goes off to the celebration, arm in arm with* CLEOPATRA. THE CONTEMPORARY *follows them. The music swells.* THE PRINCE, *left alone, turns to the audience.*

SCENE 15

THE PRINCE. You heard it yourselves: *If* I am able to pass the final test! And I swear to you, that's the way it's gone for years now. Patience! Over and over—patience, be patient, be patient! And always this talk about the Great Order and the True Order, which is going to make us all happy, of the Final Order, which is coming soon—*if* I am able to pass the final test! It's the old song, you know, the song of the Leaders—they can do everything except die. They drink milk and don't smoke, they take good care of themselves, until finally one finds oneself—you will come to understand my generation!—thinking of overthrowing the government. [*Laughter from the company within.*] And meanwhile where is the Princess—my betrothed?

SCENE 16

The company of masqueraders passes across the stage again. L'Inconnue de la Seine *is going about with a little basket distributing masks.*

L'Inconnue. A cotillion, gentlemen, a cotillion!

Napoleon. I must not return, they say! I *must* not! The Era of Great Leaders is past. What sort of nonsense is that? I *will* return. I will lead them against Russia——

L'Inconnue. A cotillion, sir?

Philip. Not return! He said the same to me. Freedom of thought? Insane dreamer! At least, this is a novel idea, but, good heavens!——

L'Inconnue. If I may, sir?

Philip. Yes? What are we to do now?

L'Inconnue. Don't you know, sir, what a cotillion is? You are to dance with that mask which is a partner to your own.

Philip. What? Dance? With a death's-head?

L'Inconnue. Try it again.

Philip. Ah.

L'Inconnue. Again a death's head!

Philip. Is the entire court to enjoy this performance?

Don Juan *stops with* Columbus.

Don Juan. You see: it's a dance of death. Didn't I say so? We are lost, Captain, if we don't get there.

Columbus. Where?

Don Juan. When I think of your world: Marco Polo, who discovered China, and it was as though he had arrived on the other side of time and space; Vasco da Gama; and you—ah, that was a world open in all directions, surrounded by mystery. There were islands which no human had ever set foot on, continents undiscovered by man, coasts of hope. A twig floating upon the sea was a twig of promise. Anything was possible, and everything; the earth was like a bride. There was poverty, too, I know, injustice, hunger, the tyranny of kings, but also (and as a result): Hope! There were fruits which belonged to no man, Paradise which was not yet lost—an answer to my longing. The Unknown was still possible; adventure was in the air. A virginal world. And the earth was not what it is today: a globe cut up into sections once and for all, a big ball that sits at one's elbow upon the writing desk, complete, contained, devoid of hope! For man is everywhere, and everything that we have now discovered has served to make the world, not greater, but smaller. . . . Let's fly, Captain! In seven days (or four, or less—I don't know any more) we can circle the entire world, and all those spaces that represented Hope to you will become transmuted into time, which we no longer need, for we—we have no more hope, we have no Beyond!—if you don't give it back to us, Captain.

Columbus. And where, my dear young man, am I to find it?

Don Juan. Discover it!!

Columbus. So that they can call it *America* again?

L'INCONNUE *comes forward.*

L'Inconnue. A cotillion, my lords, a cotillion?

Don Juan. Death's-heads, nothing but death's-heads.

L'Inconnue. The young gentleman sounds as though he were in despair.

Don Juan. Yes, indeed, I am—so we all are, those of us who are young——

Columbus. There is no need to be.

L'Inconnue. Really?

Columbus. The India that I meant to find is still undiscovered.

Don Juan. India?

Columbus. There still remains for you, young man, the continent of your own soul, the adventure of truth. I never saw any other regions of hope.

SCENE 17

MEE LAN *now appears. She is wearing a contemporary evening dress, which draws every eye toward her and produces a sudden silence.*

MEE LAN. Where is The Contemporary?

THE PRINCE *falls on one knee before her.* THE MASKERS *disappear.*

The Prince. Daughter of our Great Exalted Emperor, Mee Lan, which means: Beautiful Orchid——

Mee Lan. Yes, yes—I know.

The Prince. —at your chaste feet, the Brave Prince, Wu Tsiang, kneels—he who woos you truly, who has fought and won for love of you in the thick of battle, who has done all things for love of you——

Mee Lan. So I hear.

The Prince. —without thought of peril—

Mee Lan. Stand up.

The Prince. —returning home as victor, unconquered by the enemy, but conquered only by your love, returning home to kiss your chaste feet!

While THE PRINCE *kisses her feet,* MEE LAN *is looking all around for* THE CONTEMPORARY; THE MASKERS *have gone, the stage is empty.*

Mee Lan. Please. What's the good of all that Chinese nonsense? I'm looking for someone else——

The Prince. Mee Lan?

Mee Lan. It's urgent. [THE PRINCE *jumps up and stands blocking her way.*] Let me go. Seriously. This is urgent.

The Prince. Mee Lan!

Mee Lan. You make me sorry for you. What do you want? I see that you have survived the war. All right. Congratulations.

The Prince. Mee Lan?

Mee Lan. Speaking very frankly, you give me a pain.

The Prince. Don't you remember the night before I went away? The moon was shining, the full moon, and we sat here in the park——

Mee Lan. And there was some kissing. I know. I was there.

The Prince. Mee Lan——

Mee Lan. I remember too that whenever you couldn't think of anything else you always used to say: Mee Lan! Mee Lan! Mee Lan! [THE PRINCE *tries to kiss her.*] Stop that! [THE PRINCE *lets go of her and steps back, proud and sulky.*] Now you are insulted again. I remember you always get insulted when you can't think of anything else to say or do. [*She strokes his helmet.*] Come. Not another word now!

The Prince. Mee Lan—?

Mee Lan. I was a child. I'm sorry. I didn't know what love means. But then who doesn't misuse and misunderstand that word? Simply because the moon is shining. Isn't it true? One lets oneself go, simply because nobody else is at hand at the moment. And since one sometimes believes that no other man will ever appear—well, all these things are not altogether lies.

The Prince. And now another man has appeared?

Mee Lan. I was a child, an inexperienced girl. Word of honor! And then one morning—it's quite natural: I fell in love with your new helmet (the way girls nowadays fall in love with a Porsche or a Mercedes), then one morning I awoke to discover I didn't believe in princes any more.

The Prince. Now he has appeared?

Mee Lan. I hope so—yes. I hope so, very, very much—yes, oh, yes! [THE PRINCE *draws his Chinese saber.*] What does this mean . . . ? Let me go . . . I mean it. Let me go. . . . Are you disappointed, is that it . . . ? What can I do for you . . . ? I don't want to insult you; I just don't love you. . . . Why so grim? You have all my best wishes for your future career. . . . Are you trembling with self-pity, Hero of Liautung?

The Prince. He will learn to know me better!

Mee Lan. Who?

The Prince. So this is my reward! This!

Mee Lan. I don't understand you.

The Prince. I trusted in him. Who promised me fortune and success? I fought for him.

Mee Lan. Without thought of peril, I know.

The Prince. Laugh now! We are not yet at the end.

Mee Lan. You are speaking of Papa?

The Prince. Go ahead! Laugh!

Mee Lan. What did you think?

The Prince. I thought an Emperor's word could be trusted.

Mee Lan. Now you are really talking like a Chinese prince.

The Prince. It was I who won the victory!

Mee Lan. Who denies it?

The Prince. I! I! No one else!

Mee Lan. You're sure to get a medal.

The Prince. A *medal!!?*

Mee Lan. Is that what you really thought: that I would be the reward to hang on your breast?

The Prince. I will not be cheated!

Mee Lan. Who is cheating you? You fought for the Emperor of China; what does that have to do with my love? I don't love you; what does that have to do with the Emperor of China? You are really comical.

The Prince. Laugh!

Mee Lan. What do you expect to do with that sword?

The Prince. Go on! Laugh.

Mee Lan. You imagine you've been cheated, whereas you've simply been told the bare truth. That's what it is. Fighting the bloodiest battles is easier for you, Hero of Liautung, than listening to the common, everyday truth spoken in confidence.

The Prince. Laugh!

Mee Lan. I'm not laughing at all.

The Prince. The laugh will be on you, now——[*He resheathes his sword and starts out.*]

Mee Lan. Where are you going?

The Prince. At this moment, the people are at the gates.

Mee Lan. So I've heard.

The Prince. I am to disperse them.

Mee Lan. And?

The Prince. And? If I don't disperse them? If I do not protect that empire which does not reward my faith? If I open the very gates before which the people clamor?

Mee Lan. I understand.

The Prince. I will not be cheated!

Mee Lan. You've said that already. . . .

They fall silent together.

The Prince. I am going to do it.

Mee Lan. I will never be your happiness.

The Prince. And if I force you to it?

Mee Lan. That is all I can say: I will never be your happiness. [THE PRINCE *kneels again.*] Why don't you go?

The Prince. Mee Lan——

Mee Lan. I don't love you.

The Prince. For the last time——

Mee Lan. I don't love you.

The Prince. Mee Lan!

Mee Lan. You are laughable. Go away. You believe in power, all experience to the contrary. You believe in happiness through power. You make me sick. You are stupid. [A *fanfare.*] Go away! [*Another fanfare.*] The members of the court are coming. The farce is going on. . . .

SCENE 18

Entry of MANDARINS *and* EUNUCHS; *grand procession to the Royal Court (choreography, drums, music), during which* THE PRINCE, *after some irresolution, stands up and goes away.* THE MASKERS *appear, in the meanwhile, and finally* THE EMPEROR, *in full regalia.*

HWANG TI. Mandarins of my realm! I have called you together, as so many times in the past, to give me the benefit of your collective wisdom. I am handing over to your court my last adversary, a man who calls himself The Voice of the People. Let wisdom rule! As for me, my faithful subjects, I will remain silent, otherwise it might be thought that I was trying to influence this court. Let that never be thought! I will remain silent. [HWANG TI *seats himself on his throne.*]

Da Hing Yen. Bring in the prisoner! [*Drum roll.*]

Mee Lan. Papa!—

Hwang Ti. Don't interrupt now! What's the meaning of this costume?

Mee Lan. The Prince——

Hwang Ti. Later! Later!

Mee Lan. Listen to me, Papa——

Hwang Ti. Later!

A *ceremony has begun:* DA HING YEN *and four* MANDARINS *stand up, each holding a large book open before him.*

Da Hing Yen. Let us read, as the ceremony prescribes, the sentences from the handbook of ritual: "Li Gi, the Master, Spake."

First Mandarin. "The Master spake: When the path of righteousness is followed upon the earth, then it will happen that there will come forth a Son of Heaven, one who well deserves that name."

Da Hing Yen. "It was not so, however, during the Tsin Dynasty."

Second Mandarin. "The Master spake: It is of no importance how great the kingdom may be, but rather that the ruler is able to win the hearts of his subjects."

Da Hing Yen. "It was not so, however, during the Tsin Dynasty."

Third Mandarin. "The Master spake: If there is justice in the hearts of the rulers, then state and house will flourish and prosper; if the rulers are pure in heart, there will be no strife among the people, and no unrest need arise."

Da Hing Yen. "It was not so, however, during the Tsin Dynasty."

Fourth Mandarin. "The Master spake: Justice is the root of true prosperity. But if men set prosperity at any cost as a goal, evil results."

Da Hing Yen. "This, however, is how it was during the Tsin Dynasty: The rulers did not act according to justice and propriety, and the life of the people was not harmonious. People sought only for news of victories; the rulers were covetous of possessions; the strong were only concerned with cunningly hoarding their strength. They had a book of ritual, but the rulers did not live in accord with its precepts. The Prince had been placed on the throne by a eunuch who taught him how to prosecute all his enemies in mock trials. The most learned men of the court were assailed as dissidents and traitors, and no one dared to speak out against this injustice. Heaven however will always punish an unjust ruler, through the actions of his own people.

They close their books and resume their seats.

Mee Lan. Papa——

Hwang Ti. Ssssh!

Mee Lan. You will be sorry if you don't listen to me——

Hwang Ti. Be quiet!

Mee Lan. The Prince, Papa, the Prince is going to open the gates——[*Drum roll.*]

Da Hing Yen. The accused!

*The prisoner is brought in—*WANG, *the mute son of the Prologue. Helpless and uncomprehending, he turns the wrong way and gapes out at the audience.* HWANG TI *involuntarily starts up, but then sinks down again.*

Da Hing Yen. Here! Here! You must face us!

Hwang Ti. Go on!

Da Hing Yen. Accused, you are suspected of being the man who calls himself Min Ko, The Voice of the People, whose words are known to all. I ask in the name of Justice, do you know the words I refer to?

The Contemporary. For example:

"What do we count on the day of victory,
We, the farmers and folk in the land?
We count our dead, we count our dead,
While you jingle your gold in your hand."

Or——

Hwang Ti. Enough!

The Contemporary.

"He who sits on the throne:
He hopes the future never comes;
He who loves the Lord:
He hears the future in the drums."

Hwang Ti. We're not interested in hearing all these rhymes!

The Contemporary. I can well understand that, Your Majesty. Their literary value is slight. So slight that one wonders at the extraordinary price Your Majesty has placed upon their heads.

Da Hing Yen. I ask in the name of Justice: Are you the man who invented these words and spread them from mouth to mouth through the entire realm?

The Contemporary. He's not.

Hwang Ti. Silence!

The Contemporary. But I happen to know that——

Da Hing Yen. If you remain silent, my boy, that means that you do not want to be recognized. If you do not want to be recognized, that means that you must be the man we are seeking. And *that* means: Your head on the block! Therefore I ask: Do you confess to the charge or do you deny it? [WANG *shakes his head.*] You don't deny it? [WANG *nods vigorously.*] You confess? [WANG *shakes his head.*] Your Majesty, the accused denies——

Hwang Ti. We will prove him guilty! Go on!

Da Hing Yen. As you will, Your Majesty.

The Contemporary. You are innocent, I know. Why don't you speak out? They are afraid of your silence. Don't you see that? They suspect that you are thinking the truth, my son, simply because you *don't* speak.

Hwang Ti. Go on!

The Contemporary. Don't be silent, my boy, glorify them at the top of your lungs!

Hwang Ti. Go on! Are we assembled to listen to the prattlings of a court fool? Go on!

Da Hing Yen. It's an ancient custom, Your Majesty, that the man who defends the innocent before the lords of our land should be the Court Fool.

Hwang Ti. The innocent?

Da Hing Yen. In the eyes of a fool, of course, Your Majesty. We will demonstrate the opposite.

Hwang Ti. So I hope.

Da Hing Yen. As you will, Your Majesty. [*He makes a sign.*] Fu Chu, the Executioner!

In the brief pause which now occurs as they await the appearance of the executioner, two more MASKERS *appear and promenade across the stage: Schiller's* MARY STUART *and* PONTIUS PILATE.

Pilate. But then as I sat in the seat of judgment (which is called in Hebrew: Gabbatha), I answered and spake unto him: What is truth?

Da Hing Yen. Quiet!

Pilate. There was, though, an outcry before the place of judgment, and the high priests cried out and said: "Away with him! Crucify him!" Then I flogged him, but when I saw that this was accomplishing nothing, I took some water and washed my hands before the people, saying: "I am innocent of the blood of this just man."

Da Hing Yen. Quiet!

Pilate. The other man was named Barabbas and was a robber——

Da Hing Yen. Quiet!

Pilate. —or a murderer——

The Chinese executioner enters.

Da Hing Yen. Fu Chu, the Executioner! [MEE LAN *covers her face with her hands.*] Let us continue in the name of Justice. Since the accused refuses to be accused and is not willing to incriminate himself——

The Contemporary. He is mute!

Hwang Ti. Silence.

The Contemporary. I know it.

Da Hing Yen. Mute?

The Contemporary. I can't help it, Your Majesty. It's a joke, really—you have sought out The Voice of the People in order to silence him, and now you have arrested—look—a mute!

Hwang Ti. How do you know this?

The Contemporary. Any man who sees your Justice and remains silent instead of praising your Justice in order to escape from your Justice *must* be a mute, it seems to me, or else a saint who is looking for martyrdom. Are you a saint? [WANG *shakes his head.*] The accused denies being a saint.

Hwang Ti. Anyone can deny that!

The Contemporary. Except, of course, a saint. For if he is a saint, he can't lie, simply because he *is* one. Er—does Your Majesty follow the logic? Any man who sees your Justice in silence and is not posing can only be a saint or a mute, since, however, it's quite clear the accused is not a saint——

HWANG TI *stands up.*

Hwang Ti. The rack will teach him how to speak!

The Contemporary. And what shall he speak, Your Majesty?

Hwang Ti. The truth!

The Contemporary. What for?

Hwang Ti. Do you think I don't recognize the truth?

The Contemporary. So much the better, Your Majesty; then we won't need any rack.

HWANG TI *stares about him like a caged beast.*

Hwang Ti. Mute? Now all at once? How can this be? After he has mocked me in every street and village square for ten years? Am I never, never to—— [*He turns to the* MANDARINS.] Haven't I taught my judges how to conduct trials properly?

Da Hing Yen. To be sure, Your Majesty.

Hwang Ti. Go on! I say. Or am I now to be mocked at by a mute? Go on! [*He sits down again.*]

The Contemporary. You see, my boy, how much simpler it would have been if you could have at least feigned respect, as everyone else does. Your silence is ruining everything. You'll wind up forcing them to speak the truth themselves.

Da Hing Yen. Let us continue in the name of Justice. Accused! Your death sentence is prepared, and the Emperor, whose graciousness is dear to us, awaits your confession. For it is an old Chinese custom that no death sentence should be executed without proof or confession of guilt. Therefore why are you silent? If you refuse to confess that you are guilty of high treason, then in effect you are saying that the Son of Heaven, who is always in the right, is *not* in the right—and you are then for *that* reason guilty of high treason! Do you understand, my boy, what I am saying to you? In the name of Justice, although it makes no difference as far as your execution is concerned, I ask you for the last time: Do you confess to the crime of high treason or do you deny it? [WANG *shakes his head.*] That means: you deny it? [WANG *nods.*] That means: you confess? [WANG *shakes his head.*] It is not becoming for you to shake your head at this court, my boy. Answer! I ask you for the last time: Do you confess or deny your guilt? [WANG *nods and shakes his head and nods, faster and faster.*] To the dragons with you! I give up! Or—are you *really* mute? [WANG *nods.*] Your Majesty . . .

HWANG TI *springs off his throne.*

Hwang Ti. Torture him! That's not true! Torture him! That's a lie, like everything else he has already said! Torture him!

The Contemporary. What has he already said, Your Majesty?

Hwang Ti. You traitor, you wretch, you hard-hearted beast! Do you think we don't know what you are thinking behind your dirty forehead, you gaping fool, you ragamuffin, you man of the streets! The Great Wall, you say, nothing but a business deal! Millions dead, because of a business deal! Deny it, if you can! [WANG *is silent.*] Bloodsucker, you say—my whole court, a company of bloodsuckers! Do you think I haven't heard? I, Tsin She Hwang Ti, the liberator of the people, the bringer of peace, I, a bloodsucker, you say—I suck the blood of the poor, I enjoy the fruits of your labor! *Your* labor! [HWANG TI *attempts a scornful laugh.*] Ha! Ha! [WANG *is silent.*] Gape at me, yes, and tremble! I'll force you to be silent, you chatterbox, you seditionist, and if you refuse to bring one word out of your stinking throat—I know what your kind thinks! I am not the Savior of the Fatherland. I am a robber of the people, a murderer of the people, a criminal—deny it if you can! [WANG *is silent.*] You don't deny it!? [WANG *is silent.*] You dare—to my face—a criminal!—you dare—before all the mandarins of my court—to my very face! I, the mightiest man in the world, I, you say, I: a coward, a laughable simpleton, an idiot, a scarecrow of my own fear, you say, I tremble and shake, I don't dare hear what my loyal subjects really think, for I know that they hate me, you say, and there's not an honest man in my empire, you say, who wouldn't like to spit in my face if he could—— [HWANG TI *turns toward his court, suddenly composed and smiling.*] My loyal subjects, is that true? I ask you in all honesty, is there a man in this assemblage who would like to spit in my face? [BRUTUS *steps forward.*] I mean, among my *contemporaries* . . . ! [BRUTUS *steps back.*] I ask you before all the world: Is there a man who would like to spit in my face? [*They all shake their heads.*] That is to say—you love me? [*They all nod.*]

Mee Lan. Papa! Stop it! This is nonsense! Everyone knows you have the power. Papa! You're not changing the truth! Who believes you? I don't. What good is all this? Stop this farce, Papa. . . .

A silence. A MANDARIN *steps forward.*

The Mandarin. At last!

Hwang Ti. What does my loyal subject mean?

The Mandarin. Out of the mouth of your own child. At last. You have heard it.

HWANG TI *looks at him. The silence continues. Everyone stares.* HWANG TI *gives a tiny sign to* DA HING YEN. DA HING YEN *gives the same sign to* FU CHU, *who relays it to someone else, and* THE MANDARIN, *almost before he grasps it, is silently and almost magically removed as if on runners. No one moves; it is as if nothing had happened.*

Hwang Ti. I ask you one more time before all the world: Is it true, my loyal subjects, that you are all feigning loyalty simply because you fear my torture chamber? [*Everyone shakes his head.*] And you, man of the streets, you dare to tell me—to my very face—my power lies in my torture instruments. Well, you shall become acquainted with them, you liar, you damnable —ha! to my face! A criminal, you say, a man has to be a criminal to stay *out* of my prisons. And whoever is wise had better stay under cover. What do you know about wisdom, you nasty-nose? And I, you say, I kill all wisdom, I am the lie in person, I am the plague enthroned, and whoever stretches his hand toward me, it stinks of carrion; I am no Son of Heaven and no man, I am the spiritual sickness of my time—deny it, if you can! [WANG *is silent.*] You can't deny it!! [WANG *is silent.*] Shall I strangle you with my own hands, you—you *talker?* So that you are finally silenced, you with your wisdom, you Voice of the People, do you think I am going to be mocked at on the day of my victory—do you think——[HWANG TI *suddenly has a thought.*] Do you have a father? [WANG *nods, then shakes his head.*] What does that mean?

The Contemporary. His father was killed in your last war.

Hwang Ti. Do you have a mother? [WANG *nods, beaming.*] Then I will have your mother tortured—! [WANG *falls on his knees, unable to cry out.*] Fu Chu! [*The executioner steps forward.*] Is it true, Executioner, what this slanderous dog tells in every street and village square in the empire? I am the murderer of my friends, he says. I ask you, Hangman, before all the world: Of all the people you have tortured, was a single one of them a friend of mine? [FU CHU *shakes his head.*] You hear that? (HWANG TI *kicks the mute.*] Voice of the People—*you*—you hear? [MEE LAN *sobs loudly.*] Enough. The truth, I think, has been demonstrated. I, Tsin She Hwang Ti, a bloodsucker, I fatten myself on your labor! I: the murderer of my friends, the destroyer of my people—I force them into the wars, you say this to my face! I create the wars myself, you say, in order to divert the people's rage toward others and to save myself through their patriotism—in my very face! Do you think I am going to let you drag our most sacred beliefs through the mud? Our wars, our battles for peace? The barbarian dogs of the steppes, you say—they wouldn't have done anything to us if I hadn't attacked them. How do you know that? How do you know what no one can know, you gaping lout who can't even read a newspaper, you water-carrier, you mule-driver, you ragamuffin, how do you know what would have happened if I hadn't attacked just in time—attacked! Yes, indeed! Naturally, I attacked them! [HWANG TI *grows angrier.*] Shut up! I say. Shut up! [HWANG TI *seizes him and shakes him.*] One word more and I'll strangle you! One word more! [HWANG TI *hurls him to the floor.*] Thousands, hundreds of thousands, you say, slaughtered for a lie, bled white, crippled for the kingdom of spiritual sickness in our time—mine!—bled white, you say, for me! For a criminal! And this today—on the day of our victory! Do you think I am going to let you mock at all of them, the heroes of my army, thousands and hundreds of thousands, who have died for me—for *me*, yes! for *me!* [HWANG TI *is now almost voiceless.*] Shut up! I say. [*He totters back to his throne, hoarse and shaking.*] Torture him! He is the one. Torture him till he confesses. I will never listen to him. Torture him till he hears the cracking of his own bones!

FU CHU, *the executioner, drags out the mute.*

I've gotten overexcited, gentlemen of the court. You heard the slandering liar, though—enough! No more of him! He was our final adversary. My loyal subjects, assembled in honor of this glorious day, let us now proceed to the joyous banquet!

HWANG TI *rises with an effort. Music begins. Arm in arm with* CLEOPATRA, *he goes out, followed by his entire court, again with appropriate choreography.* MEE LAN—*in evening dress—and* THE CONTEMPORARY *are left behind.*

SCENE 19

THE CONTEMPORARY. You despise me, don't you? You are disillusioned. Well, what did you expect?

DON JUAN *appears and bows to* MEE LAN.

Mee Lan. Thank you, but I don't dance the cha-cha-cha.

Don Juan [*Sadly*]. Ah. [*He bows again and withdraws.*]

Mee Lan. You knew that he was mute.

The Contemporary. Yes.

Mee Lan. And you are going to permit this mute boy to be tortured—you, who know everything?

The Contemporary. Permit?

Mee Lan. You shrug your shoulders. And that's all! Shrug the shoulders, light another cigarette—while they torture a mute to force him to scream; and you, who can speak, stand there and keep silent—and that's all!

The Contemporary. What can I do?

Mee Lan. You with your learning! Time and space are one; how comforting! Destruction of the world by heat; how exciting! And the speed of light is unsurpassable; how interesting! Energy equals mass times the speed of light.

The Contemporary. —Squared.

Mee Lan. And what's the result of all this? You with your great formulas! You shrug your shoulders while a man is flayed alive, and light another cigarette!

He is silent for a moment or two, then suddenly shouts.

The Contemporary. What can I do?! [*He automatically takes out a cigarette, then speaks very quietly.*] He will be tortured. I know. As thousands before him have been. First the thumbscrew, then the nailed whip, then the business with the block and pulleys (which tears the tendons so that he will never again be able to lift his arms), then the white-hot wire, then the bone-breakers, repeated as often as necessary—all that, I know, has been going on right up to today. And whether we cry or laugh, whether we dance, sleep, read—there is probably not a single hour that goes by today in which some man somewhere is not being tortured, flayed, martyred, disgraced, murdered. [*He takes the cigarette out of his mouth again.*] But has any intellectual ever been able to forestall destiny simply because he foresaw it? We can write books and make speeches, even angry speeches: "Why this can no longer go on!" And yet it goes on. Precisely so. Great and learned persons arise and call to mankind: "The cobalt bomb, which you are now producing, will be the end of you!"—and people go on making the cobalt bomb. [*He sticks the cigarette back in his mouth and snaps on his cigarette lighter.*] You're right, Mee Lan—to shrug the shoulders and light another cigarette, that's all someone like me can do in times like these. [*He lights his cigarette.*]

Mee Lan. Talk! Nothing but talk! [*He smokes.*] Don't you hear?

The Contemporary. What?

Mee Lan. Through all of this—don't you hear? A mute, who is being tortured till he screams! Till he screams—a helpless, defenseless creature without a voice! And you hear only your own voice? I don't want to know the things you know. Why don't you cry? You with your sterile science! Why don't you cry for him? No! I hate you!

The Contemporary. Mee Lan——

Mee Lan. I hate you! [*She throws herself into a chair.*]

The Contemporary. And you—what have you done? I see you have gotten yourself dressed up. You want to be a modern woman, I see, and yet you still expect men to perform miracles. You were there, the same as I. Why didn't you save him? You put up with it, you wept, you hoped. For what? That the others would do something, that a man would, that I would? What were you able to do? Whether man or woman, we stand here, one human being facing another, and I ask you: What did *you* do? You changed clothes. That's all. [MEE LAN *sobs.*] You hate me——

Mee Lan. Yes!

The Contemporary. I don't know what you think love is. Did you hope that I would be something for you to admire and wonder at? And what do you find? A man who is not capable of changing the world——

Mee Lan. You're no man!

The Contemporary. Otherwise I would have committed suicide on the spot, is that what you mean? Is that what you expected? It wouldn't have changed the world—for there's never any shortage of deaths!—but you would have discovered that I was a man. Dead—but a man! [*He smiles teasingly.*] And you're supposed to be a Chinese princess! [*She turns away.*] You are young. And now you are sobbing. You are very young. You know what hope is, Mee Lan, but hope is not the measure of our actions—or inactions. You don't know what the world is. . . .

Two men with cigars come in: a TAIL COAT *and a* CUTAWAY.

The Tail Coat. A cigar of distinction!

The Cutaway. Isn't it?

The Tail Coat. Have you had a chance to chat with Lohengrin?

The Cutaway. Lohengrin is here, too?

The Tail Coat. The whole cultural world!

The Cutaway. Tell me, what's he like?

The Tail Coat. Lohengrin? Not a bad fellow, if you can get him to stop singing.

The Cutaway. I've been chatting with Mary Stuart.

The Tail Coat. Ah.

The Cutaway. People always think persons like that have no culture. But they know all sorts of things. A very fine person, this Stuart! And then, as I always say: What a fine gift of conversation these classical characters have! It's a shame my wife isn't here. As she always says, she simply can't live without the classics—and she means it. [*They both nod with pompous courtesy to someone offstage.*] Do you have any inkling who this Roman is who keeps watching us all the time?

The Tail Coat. I do indeed.

The Cutaway. Really?

The Tail Coat. Also a classic character.

BRUTUS *enters, holding a newspaper rolled up like a parchment scroll.*

Brutus. A word, you citizens! If I seem sad,
Think only that the sorrow of my gaze
Goes not toward men of mediocre mind.
Consider that it is a bitter task,
The full reconstitution of the State
(The which I love, you know, more than myself),
And knowledge of these things, to freely speak,
Has cast the shades of gloom across my face.

The Tail Coat. Hm.

Brutus. The times are grave. Your evening paper here—
Which you had dropped—has roused my blood
(I understand your paper all too well!);
No longer will I stand aside, the while my heart
Buries its impulses at their birth.
What is the plan? You are, my friends,
If I have understood your paper right,

My brothers under the skin, O, businessmen,
O, friends of Rome, who love the public weal,
Love Justice as I do, and will defend
Freedom with your lives, if necessary.
Have I, friends, read your thoughts aright?

The Cutaway. Yes, yes—quite.

Brutus. My name is Brutus.

The Cutaway. Ah.

The Tail Coat. What did he say?

The Cutaway. Brutus.

The Tail Coat. Hm.

Brutus. I hear the raging mob is threatening
Justice, that most noble work of man;
Is threatening with violence the State,
And in an hour of rage endangers Freedom
(But oh, how well I understand that rage
When I see the abuse of all these things!)—
A suicidal passion of destruction!
Is it then something for the common good
(Do not conceal your thoughts from me!)
That you are planning? Hark! the shouts
Of uproar that now reach our ears—a flame
Whipped by a storm that whirls about us.
What is to come? Evil is on the march
And takes whatever path it will when men
Do not remove determinedly those things
Which harm the folk (be it a man's own friend!).
You know? Declare yourselves! What do the people
want?

The Tail Coat. Higher wages. What else?

Brutus. Think not, my friends, I am an advocate
Of nonsense when I question you—
I, enemy of mob rule as I am—

Concerning the true grounds of this uprising.

The Cutaway. Higher wages are out of the question, that's quite clear. Where will that lead us? To higher prices! But try to explain this to the mob! Apart from that, though, there is nothing to worry about; the police have the situation well in hand.

Brutus. I do not understand, my friends, the form
Your government doth take, but if I read
This paper here aright, 'tis a republic——

The Cutaway. Yes, yes—quite.

The Tail Coat. Absolutely!

The Cutaway. Yes, sir!

The Tail Coat. And we won't have any tampering with it!

Brutus. Brutus is glad to hear it.

The Tail Coat. Particularly not by labor unions and the like!

Brutus. I know not the condition of your state,
And yet I hope that these police you speak of
Are not the bodyguards of tyranny.
If this were so, oh, then, eternal God!
Then let us, brothers, let us bathe our hands
In Caesar's blood up to the very elbows.
Let us make our swords smoke red with blood!
And let us step forth in the market place
And, swinging round our heads our bloody weapons,
Cry to all the world: Rescue! Freedom! Peace!

The TAIL COAT *and the* CUTAWAY *exchange uneasy glances.*

The Tail Coat. Er—if you have no objections—we can be heard here——[*They lead their classic character aside.*]

Brutus. Give me your hands—one, then the other——

They disappear. MEE LAN *and* THE CONTEMPORARY *remain. During the* BRUTUS *intermezzo, which has crossed the forestage, they have taken no notice of the interruption.*

The Contemporary. What did you expect from me? I ask you. What did you expect? I could have saved him? Is that what you think? I only had to speak up. Voluntarily. I only had to say: "I am the man you're looking for. Release this water-carrier, for he is not The Voice of the People. He is mute. Here is my head. Yes—I, an intellectual, a somewhat ordinary intellectual, a Doctor of Jurisprudence, unmarried, temporarily unemployed (since I quit my job with the life-insurance company), occupant of a two-room apartment without bath, contributor to leading literary quarterlies (which don't pay), cigarette smoker, unaffiliated, idler in the fields of Physics, History, Theology—arrest me as The Voice of the People! Please—don't laugh! Or arrest me (in selling out your titles and honors) as The Voice of the Spirit—it's all the same; my head won't change the course of history. But take it, you hangman. Otherwise I am no man in the eyes of this girl! Have pity, hangman, and take my head off my shoulders—show this girl who I am!" [MEE LAN *arises.*] Is that what you expected from me?

Mee Lan [*Taking a cigarette*]. Will you give me a light?

The Contemporary. Can a man choose martyrdom the way he chooses a job? And yet you are right. I know! The only thing the mind can do is to offer itself as a sacrifice——

Mee Lan. Will you give me a light?

The Contemporary. You have nothing more to say?

Mee Lan. I see you talk, but I hear nothing. I only hear the mute. He is the only man in this whole stupid farce.

He takes out his cigarette lighter, but doesn't snap it on yet.

The Contemporary. Maybe I'm a coward. Otherwise I would have seen what I have to do. But I don't see it——

DON JUAN *appears and bows.*

Don Juan. This time, Princess, it's not a cha-cha-cha.

MEE LAN *accepts him, smiling.*

The Contemporary. Mee Lan . . . ? Mee Lan . . . !

MEE LAN *waltzes away with* DON JUAN.

SCENE 20

HWANG TI *comes in,* CLEOPATRA *on his arm, a glass in his hand, followed by his retinue, everyone in high spirits.*

HWANG TI. No matter, my dear child, no matter—a wall is a wall, and therefore I say—hic!—I say: Let's build one! Today, tomorrow, yesterday, eh? Why do you laugh? A wall that will protect us from the future—hic!—I believe I'm beginning to feel this drink, but the situation is grave, my dear subjects, frankly grave, and therefore I say—Cleopatra, where are you? A toast! Wan-li-chang-cheng, I say, and all that dwells within it, which is the Republic and Freedom and Culture—hic!—and that means us, and as for everything outside the wall—. My dear, faithful, loyal subjects! Let us drink to the Great Wall, as it is called in the books, my faithful subjects, one more time—brr! for a moment it seemed to me as though we were concluding an affair that already for centuries, so to speak—as though we were building a wall that—hic!—has already crumbled away—as though our future, so to speak, lay—hic!—behind us! [*He seats himself on the throne.*] A toast! [*General clinking of glasses, laughter, then a sudden silence.*] What was that? [*Machine guns are heard in the distance.*] My loyal subjects, I feel unwell. All my life I have drunk milk and fruit juice so that I might see things clearly, as a Son of Heaven should; I have never smoked, never—the better to bring about that which we call the Great Order and the Final Order——[*He starts to laugh.*] Suddenly I feel quite well again! [*Another burst of machine-gun fire.*] What *is* that?!

THE CONTEMPORARY *steps forward.*

The Contemporary. That is the revolution.

Hwang Ti. Revolution?—why—?

The Contemporary. The people, my lords, are unpredictable. And who are the people? We all are; we stand behind the curtain when the neighbor is arrested and dragged away. And we become cautious in our dealings with neighbors. But in vain. One morning (around four o'clock) they come and drag your own father away; the next wave will swallow up your own brother. And every time that the sun rises again over this land, it seems that nothing has happened. On the contrary: the newspapers tell us of a disappointing wheat crop somewhere. And friends wonder whether their friend is still living, but they don't ask too many questions, lest they themselves be dragged away. And whoever is left alive lives harmlessly, and so, in truth, there is peace in the land. And yet now comes the revolution. Why? Suddenly a bagatelle is enough to start the avalanche—a harmless creature, someone whom we don't even know, a mute boy is tortured——

Hwang Ti. Harmless?

The Contemporary. —and the people, afraid for years, rush into the streets, unafraid in memory of their dead. But the people, my lords, have no voice, unless we lend them one—one of us!

Hwang Ti. What is he talking about?

The Contemporary. Arrest me, my lords, as The Voice of the People.

Hwang Ti. Hic!

The Contemporary. Precisely.

Hwang Ti. You are Min Ko? You?

The Contemporary. As much as anyone.

Hwang Ti. He thinks I am drunk. . . .

The Contemporary. If you want to find out what the people think, don't go on torturing a mute! I will tell you. Listen to me!

HWANG TI *looks about.*

Hwang Ti. Where is Fu Chu?

Fu Chu. Here. [*The Executioner takes two strides toward* THE CONTEMPORARY.]

Hwang Ti. We are listening. Speak!

THE CONTEMPORARY *stands before a huge half-circle which* THE MASKERS *and courtiers have formed about him. He has the typical manner of speaking of an intellectual: not loud, quite informal, somewhat ill at ease, but not disconcerted or confused, from time to time smiling or toying with a cigarette to mask his nervousness, the while his seriousness shows itself throughout in his objectivity.*

The Contemporary. What I have to say to you is banal; you can read it in the papers every morning. . . . We find ourselves, my lords, in the era of the hydrogen bomb, or, as the case may be, the cobalt bomb, which means—without going any further into contemporary physics—whoever is a tyrant today, wherever he may be on this planet, is a tyrant over the whole of humanity. He holds in his hand, for the first time in the history of mankind, the means to make an end of the human race—a possibility which up to now has seemed absurd; however, when you're dealing with neurotics, nothing is really strange. [*An unbeliever laughs.*] My lords, I am not drawing up the plans for the Apocalypse. I am simply reminding you of certain medical findings which are quite well known. The investigations of the survivors of Hiroshima, for example—and bear in mind that in Hiroshima we had, so to speak, a harmless bomb, one in which only the explosive effect was considered—these investigations showed among the women a definite gene damage as a result of radioactivity, a significant aftereffect which remains at least very much open to question. I can't go any further into this matter here; it involves various horrible throwbacks in certain carriers of the genes which produce various kinds of physical deformities and mental deficiencies. The slaying of the children of Bethlehem is perhaps comparable to Hiroshima, except that

Hiroshima involved not only living children but those of the future as well—while Bethlehem, which was, to be sure, no idyl for those concerned, was of no real significance to mankind at large——[*A murmur of dissatisfaction.*] But let me be brief. For the first time in the history of man (for up till now the tyrant who sent his Rome up in flames was always simply a temporary and quite local catastrophe)—for the first time (and therefore, my lords, the example of history will help us no longer!) we are face to face with the choice, will there be a human race or will there not? The end of the world can be manufactured. Technology—no problem. The more we become able to do (thanks to technology), the more nakedly we stand, like Adam and Eve, before the primal question: "What do we want?"—before what is ultimately a moral decision. However, if we decide "The human race must live!," that means your way of making history is no longer of any importance. We can no longer tolerate a civilization which considers war unavoidable, that much is clear——

Hwang Ti. What is he saying? I am no longer of any importance—!

The Contemporary. For war means the end of everything.

Hwang Ti. Hic!

The Contemporary. And I assure you, my lords: There is no ark we can board to save us from a radioactive flood!

Hwang Ti. Does he think I am drunk? I *am* of importance! What is this radioactivity? And really—am I a monster? Why can't I have some of this radioactivity, too? Does that mean that people don't trust me? [THE CONTEMPORARY *sees that he is interrupted and falls silent.*] Am I a tyrant? [FU CHU *ostentatiously arranges his hangman's noose in order to be ready.*] Why don't you answer?

The Contemporary. So far as I know, no one who *was* a tyrant ever called himself one. The position is more desirable than the title.

Hwang Ti. Answer: Yes or no!

The Contemporary. What's this hangman doing here? Is he going to prove that I am wrong if I answer "Yes"?

Hwang Ti. Am I a tyrant?

THE CONTEMPORARY, *pausing a second, involuntarily sticks a cigarette in his mouth.*

The Contemporary. Yes.

FU CHU *throws the noose over his neck.*

Hwang Ti. Release him! [FU CHU *takes the noose away again.*] Speak further! I am going to prove you wrong. Speak further! I am a great admirer of your mental agility.

The Contemporary. I have said what I have to say.

Hwang Ti. We listen to you with pleasure.

THE CONTEMPORARY, *uncertain about this behavior of* HWANG TI, *who is smiling benignly, looks about like someone who feels he is being mocked, then suddenly speaks quietly and directly.*

The Contemporary. Smile, gentlemen, mock at me! I see what I see, what everyone who wants to see can see: I see our earth, which is no more, a planet without life, cruising through the darkness of eternity, illuminated by the sun, but no creature lives to feel the warmth of its rays, and dead is the brightness of day; I see the streaked shadows of its mountains and its violet-colored oceans—dead—clouds like silver fungi, and dead are the continents, pale as the moon, fruitless, bare—a barren, sterile star, revolving aimlessly like a million other stars. I see the cities and states of mankind, as they once were, the lost oases of time: Greece, Italy, Europe! Morning dawns, but no one is alive to see *this* morning, no bird, no child, no voice of greeting—not even a voice of lamentation. Nothing. Water, fire, and wind rage and roar, but silently, for no ear hears them. And the light—the same light as this here today: bluish in the sky, brown or green on the earth, white or purple on your walls, or yellow or red—the light is colorless! For no eye sees it. And empty and blind as his world is God, blind and empty and without creatures of His making: without the mirror of a dying human eye, without our human consciousness of time—timeless—continents, which once rose up shining out of the mists of timelessness and into the consciousness of man: Asia, Europe, America—meaningless! senseless! lifeless! spiritless! empty of man! empty of God!

Prolonged general silence.

Hwang Ti. Bravo! Bravo! Now I call that poetry! [HWANG TI *claps, and then they all clap. It mounts to an ovation, as at a concert or in the theater.*] Where is Da Hing Yen, the Master of the Revels?

Da Hing Yen. Here.

DA HING YEN *steps forward in place of the executioner.*

Hwang Ti. Read the document!

Da Hing Yen [*Unrolls a scroll*]. "What would the mightiest empire in the world, victor over all barbarians, be without the lustrous splendor and adornment of its intelligentsia? Therefore is it an ancient custom to reward and honor the wise men of our realm, to whom we always listen with pleasure. And therefore do we hereby proclaim" [*Drum roll.*] "The Kung Fu Tse Award, established by our Great Exalted Emperor, Tsin She Hwang Ti, called the Son of Heaven, he who is always in the right, annually awarded to the wise man who dares to portray the world as it was before our reign and thereby dares to be our enemy—all honor in this sacred hour to the man who was able so strikingly and movingly to speak into the ears of the tyrant of the Chinese Wall the complete and utter truth." [*Drum roll.*]

Hwang Ti. Place the golden chain about his neck! [DA HING YEN *lays a golden chain about* THE CONTEMPORARY'S *neck.*] All hail!

Hoisted onto the shoulders of the EUNUCHS, THE CONTEMPORARY *covers his face.*

All. Heil! Heil! Heil!

Cleopatra. And a kiss from me——

The jubilation changes into equally loud laughter, everyone lifts his glass, a fanfare is sounded, then a sudden scream. Silence.

SCENE 21

The revolution is here: men with arm-bands and sub-machine guns: one sees them now as the people on the stage disperse and draw back. HWANG TI, *left standing alone, continues laughing for a moment in the general silence, then stops suddenly.*

HWANG TI. Hic!—Who are you?

THE PRINCE *steps forward, now in plain trousers and white shirt.*

The Prince. There he is—your Son of Heaven! Look, he can scarcely stand——

Hwang Ti. My prince?

The Prince. I am no prince!

Hwang Ti. And in this costume—?

The Prince. Liquidate him!

The Contemporary. Stop!

The Prince. Fire!

The Contemporary. Stop! I said . . . Stop! [*He drags the Chinese mother out of the crowd of people.*] Here is the Mother! [*It is suddenly still.*] She is here to plead for the freedom of her son. [*He turns to the crowd.*] Don't you all see the game that is being played here? Our prince, who has just been playing the part of a man of the people (as is customary in military *putsches*), this born general who has sacrificed his thirty thousand men in order to spare himself for the problems of the postwar world—naturally he would welcome the idea that The Voice of the People was a mute!

The Prince. Him too! Liquidate him! All of them!

The Contemporary. How well we have come to know this

figure, so easy to see through; only the people, the unhappy people, always see through him too late. . . . The only hope left in this entire game, the last hope that I see, is you. [*He turns to the mother.*] You are the Chinese Mother, the good and poor mother who thinks that she plays no role in the history of this world. Right?

Olan. Yes, sir, yes. . . .

The Contemporary. Tell me, haven't you informed me that your son is mute?

Olan. Yes, sir, yes. . . .

The Contemporary [*Gestures toward the right*]. Bring him in.

FU CHU *brings in the tortured mute.*

Olan. Wang!!!

The Contemporary. Is this your son?

Olan. My Wang! my poor Wang—!

The Contemporary. Tell the whole world what you know, mother. Testify that he is mute.

Olan. What have they done to you, Wang? Who has broken your fingers? Who has wrenched your shoulders? My poor Wang, my dear Wang, my stupid Wang! Don't you recognize me? Who has burned your tongue? Who has torn the skin from your arms? My blood, my blood, I kiss you! You shouldn't have stood out in front of the crowd that day; you should have listened to your mother! Oh, Wang, my son! Look at me! Why don't you at least listen, if you can't speak? Oh, Wang! Oh, Wang!

The Contemporary. Control yourself.

Olan. Why have they done this to you?

The Contemporary. It will never happen again. If you speak the truth now before all of us—your son is a mute, isn't he?

Olan. Yes, sir, he is my son.

The Contemporary. He is not Min Ko, he is not the man who made up the verses. Say it!

Olan. Verses?

The Contemporary. Because he is mute!

Olan. Wang—what have you done?

The Contemporary. He has done nothing.

Olan. Wang?

The Contemporary. Testify to the truth, nothing more. Testify with a single word that he is a mute.

Olan. Have I done you an injustice, Wang? I have always thought that you were stupid. My Wang, my poor Wang! Is that true, that you have made verses?

The Contemporary. But, my good woman——

Olan. My son is not stupid!

The Contemporary. No one has claimed that.

Olan. Why shouldn't he do it? My son! Why shouldn't he make verses?

The Contemporary. It's not true——

Olan. Oh, Wang, my sweet Wang, my unhappy Wang, my son, why have you never told your mother, my proud Wang, that you are the man?

The Contemporary. It's not true!

Olan. Why shouldn't my son be a man of importance?

The Contemporary. Woman——

Olan. Yes, he is the man! Yes! Yes!

The revolutionaries break out in jubilation, the crowd lifts WANG *onto its shoulders and starts to carry him into the streets. Then—*MEE LAN *appears; it grows still once more. She stands there with disordered hair and torn clothing.*

Mee Lan. Here I am, Prince.

The Contemporary. Mee Lan?!

Mee Lan. Shamed and disgraced by the power you have unleashed. I told you once: I will never be your happiness. Well, here I am.

The Prince. Forward! [*No one stirs.*] Forward! A savior of the world cannot trouble himself over a single individual! Forward!

The Contemporary. Stop!

The Prince. Liquidate them!

The Contemporary. Stop, I say!

The Prince. All of them! All of them!

Shots; the lights go out for a moment; shouts, cries of confusion; and when the lights come back on, the scene is empty of persons. The scenery has collapsed, and the stage is seen as a stage; the machinery is visible. Distant cries of confusion and rioting in the distance. BRUTUS *and his two companions come in as if to view the ruins.*

SCENE 22

THE TAIL COAT. What do you say about this?

The Cutaway. What do you say now?

Brutus. The fury of the mob I understand,
Though it be evil: impulse, passion,
Sprung from the selfsame root as tyranny,
Despite the work of human reason.
Injustice reigns to kill injustice,
And bloodily there ends what was a hope
For freedom, right, a world of common good.

The Cutaway. That's the way it is here, all right.

Brutus. Now upon the shoulders of the angry mob,
So long neglected and suspected, now
They hoist—they, throwers-down of tyranny—
Their newest leader and their next oppressor.

The Tail Coat. At least he's a former general.

The Cutaway. That's right.

The Tail Coat. You can do business with generals, I always say.

The Cutaway. You're right.

The Tail Coat. Generals have behind them a certain tradition.

Brutus [*Aside*].
Oh you, Octavius and Mark Antony,
How often shall we meet at Philippi?

The Cutaway. What did you say?

Brutus. Nothing, nothing, I was lost in memory. . . .

The Cutaway. Well, how do you judge our present situation?

Brutus [*Aside*].
And yet I will not deal unjustly with Mark Antony;
He was an enemy of larger size than this,
One who stood in person on the field!

BRUTUS *lays his hands on their shoulders.*

I tell you: be of cheer! The form and manner
Of your business dealings, honest men,
You noble business-leaders, friends of Rome,
I know too well; haven't you proved yourselves?
I see you prosperous, well fed; what do you fear?
As for the mob, consider only this:
How can a mob like this, now here, now there,
Free itself from your bland tyranny?
If it really wants its freedom, yes! But does it?

The Tail Coat. Then you think . . . ?

Brutus. As necessary as is daily bread
Are despotism, arrogance, misrule
To you—these things that make men great.
He who freely tolerates injustice
(Look into your hearts!) then sees himself
As somehow thereby just—oh, irony!
Oft have I thought of this. . . . Is it not true?

The Cutaway. Very interesting—hmm. . . .

The Tail Coat. Yes, indeed. . . .

The Cutaway. A rather psychological interpretation. . . .

Brutus. How could it otherwise have happened
That such as you could for two thousand years
Still hold the center of the stage
Long after Caesar fell for your false sakes?

The Cutaway. You mean—?

Brutus. I mean: Be of good cheer! You'll not die out,
O noble citizens with hollow hearts!

And if one stabs you with a sudden dagger—

Suddenly he has a dagger in each hand.

(So bitter has the world converted me!)—

He plunges the daggers into their bellies.

Good cheer! As species, you will still survive!

The two men, who have listened to their classic character with growing suspicion, clutch their sides where the daggers are sticking; meanwhile, BRUTUS, *stepping forward two steps, turns to* THE CONTEMPORARY, *who now comes in from the side.*

Brutus. What is it?

The Contemporary. The play is at an end.

Brutus. The reason?

The Contemporary. Because the farce is going to start all over again; again we must repeat it——

SCENE 23

ROMEO *and* JULIET *enter as at the beginning. Music again.*

JULIET. It was the nightingale and not the lark
That pierced the fearful hollow of thine ear;
Nightly she sings on yond pomegranate tree.
Believe me, love, it was the nightingale.

Romeo. Our only hope is haste; delay is death.

Juliet. Oh, thinkst thou we shall ever meet again?

A WAITER *in tails appears, right.*

Waiter. Ladies and gentlemen: the Polonaise is beginning on the terrace. The company awaits your pleasure.

[*He disappears.*

Juliet. O God! I have an ill-divining soul;
The song of birds, the whisp'ring of the trees,
All make me fear we'll never meet again,
We pawns of love in a divided world,
By civil discord cruelly transposed.
Each look, each glance, but makes me newly fear,
As though each kiss, so sweet, were full of poison,
The fear that death is counting every kiss.
O pain of love! O pain of innocence!
So happy as we are, we also fear,
And fearfully the frailty of this world
We see. Is there no place for lovers
In this world? I want to live until the Day
Of Judgment if I can. And in that time,
No breath, no tears, no sorrow of the heart,
No bitter pangs of longing could there be
So keen to make me cry out: "No!

This world is not a lovely world! It shall not be!"
The song of birds, the whisp'ring of the trees
Still makes me glad. See, love, the shining moon!
The stars' white light is dazzling pure,
Blazing in the east. The river gleams,
A shining mirror underneath the stars,
And then the birds, chill in the frosty branches,
Loudly greet the morning's early beam.
The clouds, outlined in fire, shift and dissolve,
And soon, kissed by the dawn's first rays,
The dewdrops flash, the jewelry of the earth,
And shadows flee 'neath every bush and stone.
O day! O inconceivable rich gift!
O light! O lovely light! O morning breeze,
Waking light and hue in every flower—
Too lovely and too sweet to be endured!—
Remembrance in the sweet scent of the leaves,
The spice of berries, ah, like tender lips,
Remembrance of the rainbow-sparkling sea,
Of all this wondrous world, the great, the small,
A day of dallying with a butterfly
While lounging on my sun-warmed window-ledge;
A mute smooth stone caressed by mute smooth hands;
And one's own image shimmering in a pond;
And oh, my dear beloved's voice and face—
Remembering, of all, one single day
When fearful longing stood before my eyes
And made me cry: "O God, to live is all!"
O holy world! O world! O bitter world!
We love you so; you shall not be destroyed!

A WAITER *in tails appears, left.*

Waiter. Ladies and gentlemen: the company awaits your pleasure. [*The* WAITER *disappears.*

Romeo. If I but knew, love, where we are—and when!

A swarm of costumes, and they smell of moth balls:
It is as though they're dead, and yet they speak
And dance about and form in circles
Like little figures on a musical clock.

Juliet. Away, my love, away! and let us flee!

Romeo. But where?

THE MASKER'S *Polonaise enters. They circle about like figures on a musical clock: every figure, as he comes to the front of the stage, speaks in his turn.*

Napoleon. I must not return! they say. I must not! What is the sense in such remarks? Russia must be beaten. It was a most unusually severe winter. I will lead you against Russia. . . .

L'Inconnue. I am the girl from the banks of the Seine, the nameless one. I'm only known by my death mask; you can buy it in any second-hand shop. Nobody asks about my life. . . .

Pilate. I do not like decisions. How am I to decide what is the truth? I am innocent of the blood of this just man. . . .

Philip. I understand heretics; I have burned them by the thousands and the hundreds of thousands; I have done my duty. . . .

Don Juan. I search for Paradise. I am young. I want to be, only to be. I search for a virginal world. . . .

Brutus. Is this what History means, that ignorance
Returns forever, endlessly triumphing?
When I see this, it's like an evil dream. . . .

Cleopatra. I am Cleopatra; I am the woman who believes in victors, I love victors, I love men who make history, but, above all, I love *men!* . . .

Columbus. I don't understand it. They call it America, and they say it is not India I have discovered—not India, not the truth . . . !

Romeo. O Juliet! this night I'll lie with thee.

Juliet. O Romeo! beloved Romeo!

Romeo. How oft when men are at the point of death
Have they been merry! O my love! my wife!
The world's become a single grave! O eyes,
Look, look your last! Arms, take your last
Embrace—thus, with a kiss, I die!

Darkness, and the music ceases.

SCENE 24

In the foreground, left and right of the stage, stand MEE LAN *(with disordered hair and torn clothing) and* THE CONTEMPORARY *(with a golden chain about his neck); they look at one another.*

THE CONTEMPORARY. Look at me, the weak and the helpless!

Mee Lan. You have said what you had to say.

The Contemporary. And achieved nothing!

Mee Lan. And still you had to say it.

The Contemporary. Why? What for?

Mee Lan. This is the truth we have learned: You, the helpless, and I, the shamed and insulted, we stand here in our time, and the world rolls forward over us. This is our history. Why do you hide your face? [*She kneels before him.*] I love you. I have come to understand you, and I love you. I, the arrogant, kneel before you, the scorned and despised, and I love you. [*He is silent.*] And now it is you who are mute.

SLOW CURTAIN

DRAMABOOKS

WHEN ORDERING, please use the Standard Book Number consisting of the publisher's prefix, 8090–, plus the five digits following each title. (Note that the numbers given in this list are for paperback editions only. Many of the books are also available in cloth.)

MERMAID DRAMA BOOKS

Christopher Marlowe (Tamburlaine the Great, Parts I & II, Doctor Faustus, The Jew of Malta, Edward the Second) (0701–0)
William Congreve (Complete Plays) (0702–9)
Webster and Tourneur (The White Devil, The Duchess of Malfi, The Atheist's Tragedy, The Revenger's Tragedy) (0703–7)
John Ford (The Lover's Melancholy, 'Tis Pity She's a Whore, The Broken Heart, Love's Sacrifice, Perkin Warbeck) (0704–5)
Richard Brinsley Sheridan (The Rivals, St. Patrick's Day, The Duenna, A Trip to Scarborough, The School for Scandal, The Critic) (0705–3)
Camille and Other Plays (Scribe: A Peculiar Position, The Glass of Water; Sardou: A Scrap of Paper; Dumas: Camille; Augier: Olympe's Marriage) (0706–1)
John Dryden (The Conquest of Granada, Parts I & II, Marriage à la Mode, Aureng-Zebe) (0707–X)
Ben Jonson Vol. 1 (Volpone, Epicoene, The Alchemist) (0708–8)
Oliver Goldsmith (The Good Natur'd Man, She Stoops to Conquer, An Essay on the Theatre, A Register of Scotch Marriages) (0709–6)
Jean Anouilh Vol. 1 (Antigone, Eurydice, The Rehearsal, Romeo and Jeannette, The Ermine) (0710–X)
Let's Get a Divorce! and Other Plays (Labiche: A Trip Abroad, and Célimare; Sardou: Let's Get a Divorce!; Courteline: These Cornfields; Feydeau: Keep an Eye on Amélie; Prévert: A United Family; Achard: Essays on Feydeau) (0711–8)
Jean Giraudoux Vol. 1 (Ondine, The Enchanted, The Madwoman of Chaillot, The Apollo of Bellac) (0712–6)
Jean Anouilh Vol. 2 (Restless Heart, Time Remembered, Ardèle, Mademoiselle Colombe, The Lark) (0713–4)
Henrik Ibsen: The Last Plays (Little Eyolf, John Gabriel Borkman, When We Dead Awaken) (0714–2)
Ivan Turgenev (A Month in the Country, A Provincial Lady, A Poor Gentleman) (0715–0)
George Farquhar (The Constant Couple, The Twin-Rivals, The Recruiting Officer, The Beaux Stratagem) (0716–9)
Jean Racine (Andromache, Britannicus, Berenice, Phaedra, Athaliah) (0717–7)
The Storm and Other Russian Plays (The Storm, The Government Inspector, The Power of Darkness, Uncle Vanya, The Lower Depths) (0718–5)
Michel de Ghelderode: Seven Plays Vol. 1 (The Ostend Interviews, Chronicles of Hell, Barabbas, The Women at the Tomb, Pantagleize, The Blind Men, Three Players and a Play, Lord Halewyn) (0719–3)
Lope de Vega: Five Plays (Peribáñez, Fuenteovejuna, The Dog in the Manger, The Knight from Olmedo, Justice Without Revenge) (0720–7)
Calderón: Four Plays (Secret Vengeance for Secret Insult, Devotion to the Cross, The Mayor of Zalamea, The Phantom Lady) (0721–5)
Jean Cocteau: Five Plays (Orphée, Antigone, Intimate Relations, The Holy Terrors, The Eagle with Two Heads) (0722–3)
Ben Jonson Vol. 2 (Every Man in His Humour, Sejanus, Bartholomew Fair) (0723–1)
Port-Royal and Other Plays (Claudel: Tobias and Sara; Mauriac: Asmodée; Copeau: The Poor Little Man; Montherlant: Port-Royal) (0724–X)
Edwardian Plays (Maugham: Loaves and Fishes; Hankin: The Return of the Prodigal; Shaw: Getting Married; Pinero: Mid-Channel; Granville-Barker: The Madras House) (0725–8)
Alfred de Musset: Seven Plays (0726–6)
Georg Büchner: Complete Plays and Prose (0727–4)
Paul Green: Five Plays (Johnny Johnson, In Abraham's Bosom, Hymn to the Rising Sun, The House of Connelly, White Dresses) (0728–2)
François Billetdoux: Two Plays (Tchin-Tchin, Chez Torpe) (0729–0)
Michel de Ghelderode: Seven Plays Vol. 2 (Red Magic, Hop, Signor!, The Death of Doctor Faust, Christopher Columbus, A Night of Pity, Piet Bouteille, Miss Jairus) (0730–4)
Jean Giraudoux Vol. 2 (Siegfried, Amphitryon 38, Electra) (0731–2)
Kelly's Eye and Other Plays by Henry Livings (Kelly's Eye, Big Soft Nellie, There's No Room for You Here for a Start) (0732–0)
Gabriel Marcel: Three Plays (Man of God, Ariadne, Votive Candle) (0733–9)
New American Plays Vol. 1, ed. by Robert W. Corrigan (0734–7)
Elmer Rice: Three Plays (Adding Machine, Street Scene, Dream Girl) (0735–5)
The Day the Whores Came Out to Play Tennis . . . by Arthur Kopit (0736–3)
Platonov by Anton Chekhov (0737–1)
Ugo Betti: Three Plays (The Inquiry, Goat Island, The Gambler) (0738–X)

Jean Anouilh Vol. 3 (Thieves' Carnival, Medea, Cécile, Traveler Without Luggage, Orchestra, Episode in the Life of an Author, Catch As Catch Can) (0739–8)
Max Frisch: Three Plays (Don Juan, The Great Rage of Philip Hotz, When the War Was Over) (0740–1)
New American Plays Vol. 2 ed. by William M. Hoffman (0741–X)
Plays from Black Africa ed. by Fredric M. Litto (0742–8)
Anton Chekhov: Four Plays (The Seagull, Uncle Vanya, The Cherry Orchard, The Three Sisters) (0743–6)
The Silver Foxes Are Dead and Other Plays by Jakov Lind (The Silver Foxes Are Dead, Anna Laub, Hunger, Fear) (0744–4)

THE NEW MERMAIDS

Bussy D'Ambois by George Chapman (1101–8)
The Broken Heart by John Ford (1102–6)
The Duchess of Malfi by John Webster (1103–4)
Doctor Faustus by Christopher Marlowe (1104–2)
The Alchemist by Ben Jonson (1105–0)
The Jew of Malta by Christopher Marlowe (1106–9)
The Revenger's Tragedy by Cyril Tourneur (1107–7)
A Game at Chess by Thomas Middleton (1108–5)
Every Man in His Humour by Ben Jonson (1109–3)
The White Devil by John Webster (1110–7)
Edward the Second by Christopher Marlowe (1111–5)
The Malcontent by John Marston (1112–3)
'Tis Pity She's a Whore by John Ford (1113–1)
Sejanus His Fall by Ben Jonson (1114–X)

SPOTLIGHT DRAMABOOKS

The Last Days of Lincoln by Mark Van Doren (1201–4)
Oh Dad, Poor Dad . . . by Arthur Kopit (1202–2)
The Chinese Wall by Max Frisch (1203–0)
Billy Budd by Louis O. Coxe and Robert Chapman (1204–9)
The Devils by John Whiting (1205–7)
The Firebugs by Max Frisch (1206–5)
Andorra by Max Frisch (1207–3)
Balm in Gilead and Other Plays by Lanford Wilson (1208–1)
Matty and the Moron and Madonna by Herbert Lieberman (1209–X)
The Brig by Kenneth H. Brown (1210–3)
The Cavern by Jean Anouilh (1211–1)
Saved by Edward Bond (1212–X)
Eh? by Henry Livings (1213–8)
The Rimers of Eldritch and Other Plays by Lanford Wilson (1214–6)
In the Matter of J. Robert Oppenheimer by Heinar Kipphardt (1215–4)
Ergo by Jakov Lind (1216–2)
Biography: A Game by Max Frisch (1217–0)

For a complete list of books of criticism and history of the drama, please write to Hill and Wang, 72 Fifth Avenue, New York, New York 10011.